P9-DGV-811

MISSION:
POLAR BEAR
RESCUE

A polar bear approaches the open water of the Arctic Ocean's edge.

MISSION: POLAR BEAR RESCUE

ALL ABOUT POLAR BEARS AND HOW TO SAVE THEM

NANCY F. CASTALDO and KAREN de SEVE WITH NATIONAL GEOGRAPHIC EXPLORER DANIEL RAVEN-ELLISON

NATIONAL GEOGRAPHIC KiDS

WASHINGTON, D.C.

>>CONTENTS

6 **Foreword**

8 **Introduction**

10 **Through a Polar Bear's Eyes**

14 **Chapter 1:** Kings of the Arctic

30 **Chapter 2:** Land of Polar Bears

46 **Chapter 3:** Life Begins on the Ice

62 **Chapter 4:** Ice Hunters

78 **Chapter 5:** Polar Bears and People

92 **Chapter 6:** Take Action

106 **Conclusion**

108 **Resources**

110 **Index**

112 **Credits**

A mother polar bear relaxes with her cubs on land.

MISSION: ANIMAL RESCUE

Save ANIMALS >>> Save the WORLD

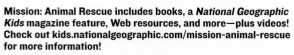

Mission: Animal Rescue includes books, a *National Geographic Kids* magazine feature, Web resources, and more—plus videos! Check out kids.nationalgeographic.com/mission-animal-rescue for more information!

MISSION: ANIMAL RESCUE

At National Geographic, we know how much you care about animals. They enrich our planet—and our lives. Habitat loss, hunting, and other human activities are threatening many animals across the globe. The loss of these animals is a loss to humanity. They have a right to our shared planet and deserve to be protected.

With your help, we can save animals—through education, through habitat protection, and through a network of helping hands. I firmly believe the animals of the world will be safer with us on their side.

Throughout this book and the other books in the Mission: Animal Rescue series, you'll see animal rescue activities just for kids. If you go online at kids.nationalgeographic.com/mission-animal-rescue, you can join a community of kids who want to help animals as much as you do. Look for animal-rescue videos, chats with explorers, and more. Plus, don't miss the dramatic stories of animal rescues in *National Geographic Kids* magazine.

We share our Earth with animals. Helping them means helping our planet and protecting our future. Together we can do it.

—Daniel Raven-Ellison, *Guerrilla Geographer and National Geographic Explorer*

YOUR PURCHASE SUPPORTS ANIMALS AND THEIR HABITATS

The National Geographic Society is a nonprofit organization whose net proceeds support vital exploration, conservation, research, and education programs. Proceeds from this book will go toward the Society's efforts to support animals and their habitats. From building bomas for big cats to protect their wild territory to studying elephants and how they communicate to exploring wild places to better understand animal habitats, National Geographic's programs help save animals and our world. Thank you for your passion and dedication to this cause. To make an additional contribution in support of Mission: Animal Rescue, ask your parents to consider texting ANIMAL to 50555 to give ten dollars. See page 112 for more information.

HELP SAVE POLAR BEARS

Nanuk, the Ice Bear. God's Dog. Great Sea Bear or Lord of the Arctic. Humans have given polar bears many names, but all show their respect and reverence. Polar bears' ability to survive in the harshest environment on Earth is what makes them stand as a symbol of strength and endurance among people across the world. Their playfulness and majesty are just two more reasons why they are the subject of story and myth. We idolize them. Yet despite their elegance and strength, global changes threaten these creatures in their Arctic habitat.

We don't want to imagine a world without them. But our world is changing, especially in the northern areas where polar bears live. The world is warming and the sea ice polar bears require for hunting is melting. Continual warming will ultimately threaten all polar bears. Some are already in trouble. Certain subpopulations, where warming has not reached serious levels, are doing well. For now . . .

Should we be concerned about polar bears? Scientists believe their future seems bleak unless we humans make changes to our behavior. However, traditional Inuit hunters feel differently and see an undiminished population. Providing hope, biologist and photographer Paul Nicklen notes that "As dire as things are, polar bears are thriving in many areas."

More study on the state of this threatened species is critically important. We need to work together to conserve these majestic creatures so that the Arctic ecosystem can flourish and future generations can enjoy polar bears as much as we do. With help, we can make a future for them.

At the end of each chapter in this book, you'll find rescue activities. By doing these activities, you'll learn more about polar bears and help share the message about the importance of these creatures. Each activity will help you learn how to help polar bears.

But don't be modest! Read on to learn how to make your voice loud. Let's help polar bears!

A polar bear crosses the Arctic ice in search of prey or a mate.

>> THROUGH A POLAR BEAR'S

Wind and snow whip across Canada's Hudson Bay to a place where three ecosystems meet—marine, tundra, and boreal forest. Slowly, across miles of frozen landscape, a huge mass of white fur lumbers toward Churchill, Manitoba—a polar bear.

His paws crunch the ice and snow below them, and he moves a bit slower than he did in previous years. Big scars cover his nose from battles with walruses and other bears on the ice.

Just as he's done every October, he arrives to the shores of Hudson Bay waiting for the icy water to freeze solid so he can return to the ice to hunt seals and other prey. Like many other polar bears, he's drawn to the Canadian town by the smells of food, the freezing ice, and the cooling temperatures. Churchill has become known as the polar bear capital of the world.

Scores of humans, visiting from all parts of the globe, spot him from the open windows of the waiting Tundra Buggies. They marvel at his large size. "That's Dancer!" someone calls out. Dancer spots the eyes on him. He hears them, too, but he's used to the attention. In fact, people in buggies intrigue him. And those smells!

Dancer settles down to survey the younger bears in the distance.

EYES

Dancer settles into the snow just yards away from the remote buggy lodge and watches the younger bears spar in the distance. They won't bother with him. They know the big guy rules! Dancer's size makes the other bears respect him and stay their distance. He's close to 25 years old, far older than most bears in the wild. He's seen many more seasons than the bears around him.

Dancer has spent the spring season hunting for seal pups hidden in snow dens. He might have eaten a walrus or two, or even a whale carcass. By the time the ice melted in July, he was fat and happy. After a summer of not having anything substantial to eat, Dancer is a little thinner and is anxious to get back out on the ice to hunt again. But it isn't quite cold enough yet.

A hush falls over the Tundra Buggy as Dancer stands on his hind legs. He easily towers over an average man. He faces the excited tourists as they peer out the windows, cameras ready. They fall silent as they watch him. What will he do?

In the early-morning light, Dancer begins to stretch his neck. He paws at the air above him, feeling its autumn crispness. Then he begins to sway back and forth in the signature style that earned him his nickname. He hears the clicks of camera shutters and the giggles and gasps from the buggy people. But that's not his focus: The coolness feels right, and the smells remind him of a full belly. Soon, Dancer will eat tasty seal fat, but for now he settles back down and watches the people in the buggy and the bears all around him. Dancer will wait for the coolness to spread and for the chill to freeze the ice solid. Then he will be able to return to his winter kingdom.

Dancer standing in the signature style that helped earn his nickname

Younger bears respect Dancer and keep their distance.

THERE ARE
BETWEEN 900 AND
1,000 POLAR BEARS
IN THE WESTERN
HUDSON BAY AREA.

CHAPTER 1

>> KINGS OF THE ARCTIC

"THE POLAR BEAR IS LIKE THE LION OF THE NORTH. IT IS THE KING."

—GABRIEL NIRLUNGAYUK, INUIT REPRESENTATIVE

Standing atop a floating iceberg off the
coast of Alaska in the Beaufort Sea,
a polar bear scans the frozen water for prey.

POLAR BEAR PAWS ARE ABOUT 12 INCHES (30 CM) WIDE.

Polar bear paws look a little bit like human hands covered by thick, furry gloves.

Polar bears are one of nature's marvels. They live at the top of the world and seem to appear suddenly out of the snow and ice around them. They are unlike other bears, differing in both habit and appearance.

KINGS OF THE ARCTIC

Polar bears—weighing more than half a ton (454 kg)—lumber silently through the ice and snow. They live in the cold Arctic, but because they are so well insulated, they don't have a problem staying warm. Their challenge is keeping cool. As mammals, polar bears are warm-blooded and have hair on their bodies. Females give birth to live young and feed their babies milk they produce themselves.

A polar bear body is shaped differently from other bears—it's very long. Just take a look at a polar bear's neck. Its length is designed to help them swim and stick their heads into holes in the ice to search for prey. And when they find prey, their sharp cheek teeth act as little knives that can rip off chunks of meat. The polar bear's canine teeth are widely spaced and long, enabling them to grab hold of their prey.

Unlike other bears, polar bears are classified by scientists as marine mammals. British zoologist Constantine John Phipps described the bears in 1774 and gave them the scientific name *Ursus maritimus,* Latin for "maritime bear." Polar bears rely on the sea, like walruses, sea lions, whales, and other marine mammals.

Most marine mammals are truly aquatic, meaning they live and feed in the water and come to the surface mainly to breathe. Arctic marine mammals, like ringed seals, haul themselves out of the water to rest and give birth on the ice. Polar bears live on the surface of the ice but can dive and swim. They are called marine mammals because they are dependent on the sea for their food, not because they spend most of their time in the water.

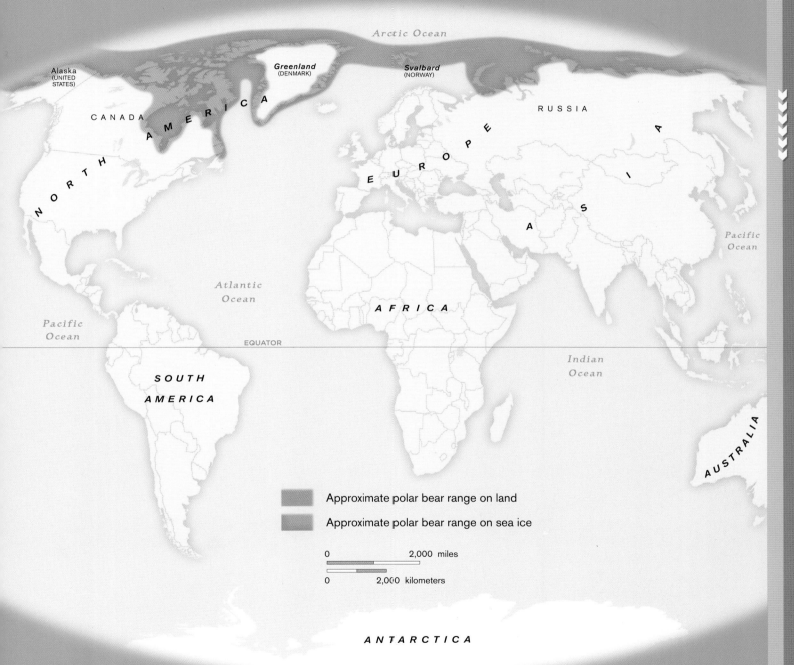

Arctic Ocean

Alaska
(UNITED
STATES)

Greenland
(DENMARK)

Svalbard
(NORWAY)

CANADA

NORTH AMERICA

RUSSIA

EUROPE

ASIA

Pacific
Ocean

Atlantic
Ocean

AFRICA

Pacific
Ocean

EQUATOR

Indian
Ocean

SOUTH
AMERICA

AUSTRALIA

Approximate polar bear range on land

Approximate polar bear range on sea ice

0   2,000 miles

0   2,000 kilometers

ANTARCTICA

WORLD-FAMOUS KNUT

When four-year-old Knut died suddenly in the Berlin Zoo, questions arose about keeping polar bears in captivity. Knut gained fame when he was rejected by his mother as an infant and was hand-raised by zookeeper Thomas Doerflein. The keeper moved into the zoo to feed him every two hours and care for him.

Knut became the first bear to live past infancy at the Berlin Zoo, making him an instant celebrity. Knutmania swept the world and Germany added a postage stamp in his honor. But even with all the excitement, Knut's existence at the zoo was always full of controversy.

Animal activists believed humans should not have raised him and that his rearing at the zoo was against animal-protection legislation.

Others pointed to the fact that polar bears live 15 to 20 years in the wild, but male polar bears have been able to live 30 years in captivity without the stresses they encounter in the wild. Unfortunately, Knut did not have that long life. He died suddenly at four years old from natural causes. He left behind a grieving city and a world made more aware of these majestic bears.

CONSTRUCTED FOR COLD

Arctic air temperatures can drop to minus 40°F (-40°C). Polar bears have evolved key features that keep them from turning into ice statues in the extreme cold: fur and fat. They have few body parts exposed to the cold. Their ears are small, and they have short tails. Their feet are big and furry for warmth and traction on the slippery ice. Their front paws are so massive polar bears can use them as snowshoes on the snow or paddles in the water. The paws can also serve as powerful weapons as they hunt for seals, their main food.

TOTALLY TUBULAR FUR

A polar bear's creamy white fur is denser than a brown bear's and is the first line of insulation against the wind, snow, and icy water. Close to the bear's skin is a two-inch (5-cm) layer of short, woolly, insulating underhair that traps air, keeping the bear warm. The next layer is made up of thin, clear, hollow guard hairs that can grow up to six inches (15 cm) long. Although this double coat of fur provides good insulation in cold

>> ANIMAL RESCUE!

POLAR BEAR PHOTO SHOOT   <<<

Founded in 1992, Polar Bears International (PBI) is the only conservation group that focuses solely on polar bears. PBI supports scientific research, creates protection measures, and teaches the public about these beloved bears. What started as a passion for photographing polar bears has become an international effort to help protect the bears in their natural habitat.

PBI knows that one of the best ways to help the bears is to get people involved. A new "citizen science" program does just that by enlisting tourists. Visitors to polar bear country can learn how to snap photos of the bears to help researchers compare the body condition and number of cubs to similar photos going back to the 1980s. Long-term studies have shown that bears in much of the western Hudson Bay were fatter and had more cubs in the 1970s and 1980s—when Arctic ice was intact—than they do now. Ultimately, PBI hopes to expand this program to other parts of polar bear territory around the world.

air, polar bears rely more on the layer of fat under their skin to keep them warm in the frigid Arctic water.

Polar bears molt every year in the warmer summer months and then grow a new coat in time for the colder temperatures. During the molting process, which can take several weeks, the bears lose only some of their fur at a time. They are never without fur. Losing some of that thick, insulating fur helps keep their body temperature regulated as the weather gets warmer.

Even though we see polar bears as white, their fur is actually transparent. It has no pigment of its own. We see it as white because it scatters the white light of the sun. On the sea ice, polar bears can range in color from white to a yellowish or creamy color depending on the cleanliness of their fur. They can also look blue-gray in early-morning light or under an overcast sky, or pink under a setting sun. These different shades appear because their colorless fur reflects and scatters visible light.

That white or off-white color makes it difficult to track polar bears on the sea ice. White bears are so well camouflaged against the snow-and-ice environment that traditional aerial photography is unsuccessful. They blend in!

Even infrared photography—which can detect heat in darkness—is a challenge. Researchers cannot see the polar bear's body because the bear's effective insulation doesn't allow enough heat to be released for the photographs. They radiate most of their heat from their faces because the hair is short there and there is little fat. Sometimes the footprints they just made in the snow show up as well as the bear itself!

WARM AND INSULATING FAT

A fat bear is a warm bear. Just like the insulation inside the walls of a house, the fat keeps the cold out and the heat in. Polar bears have two to four inches (5 to 10 cm) of fat beneath their black skin that provides insulation and keeps their large bodies afloat in the water. Even though the bears have such a thick fur coat, it is the fat that keeps them warm in the water. Wet fur does not insulate well, and mother bears try their best to keep their young, lean cubs out of the freezing water.

POLAR BEAR SPOTLIGHT
MONITORING POLAR BEARS

Scientists track and monitor polar bears in a variety of ways. These tools provide scientists with the information they need to study polar bear populations.

Bears are tattooed on the inside of their upper lip with an identification number.

ANIMAL SUPERPOWERS

POLAR BEAR MYTHS

POLAR BEARS AND PENGUINS DO NOT LIVE TOGETHER.

THERE ARE NO POLAR BEARS IN ANTARCTICA.

POLAR BEARS ARE NOT LEFT-HANDED. THEY USE BOTH PAWS.

POLAR BEARS DO NOT USE BLOCKS OF ICE TO KILL THEIR PREY.

Glue-on and ear-tag satellite transmitters are being tried on male polar bears by the U.S. Fish and Wildlife Service.

Female bears can wear a tracking collar around their necks. Males can't be fitted with these because their necks are as wide as their heads, allowing the collar to easily slip off.

POWERFUL PAWS

Thick hair insulates toes and adds extra traction.

Curved claws hook food and assist in den digging and ice breaking.

Thick footpads with bumps, called papillae, improve grip on slippery ice.

Large, wide paws act as snowshoes, preventing bears from sinking into deep Arctic snow.

Very large front paws act as paddles when swimming.

A polar bear prowls the Arctic pack ice in search of seals during the summer thaw.

The fat even helps polar bears survive through the months when they are in between meals. It provides stored-up energy for the bear. Polar bears that have been successful hunters have lots of fat, and therefore lots of stored energy.

READING THE SIGNS

As the apex indicator species for the Arctic ecosystem, polar bears serve an important role. The health of their population indicates the health of the entire ecosystem. If they are healthy, the ecosystem is healthy. If they suffer at all, the ecosystem is most likely also suffering. They are like a signal that says, "Hey, something's wrong here!" We would not have polar bears if all the pieces of the ecosystem and food web beneath them were not working properly.

In addition to serving as an indicator species, polar bears contribute to the ecosystem itself. It is possible that without them the Arctic ecosystem could crumble. According to some scientists, a "trophic cascade"—a complete uncoupling of the Arctic food chain—is possible with a decline in the polar bear population.

There are an estimated 21,000 species of plants and animals in the Arctic. Many of those species rely on polar bears for their survival. Arctic foxes, for example, feed on the seal carcasses that polar bears leave behind after they eat. If polar bears were not eating seals, the seal population would increase and become unhealthy. The fox population would also suffer from lack of food. Even humans would suffer from the disrupted balance because we also depend on many of the species required for a healthy Arctic ecosystem.

A MELTING WORLD

Earth's atmosphere acts like a greenhouse. Water vapor, carbon dioxide (CO_2), and methane are the primary "greenhouse gases." These gases occur naturally and capture some of the heat energy reflected from Earth. Greenhouse gases usually enable the atmosphere to

(continued on p. 26)

>>> ANIMAL RESCUE!

<<<

THE WHISKERS HAVE IT

Biological science professor Jane Waterman looks at the behavior of polar bears in Churchill, Manitoba. Her lab has developed a noninvasive whisker-pattern identification method to study the bears. Photographs taken of the bears in western Hudson Bay enable the scientists to study the details of each spot pattern. By looking at a photograph and placing a grid of lines on top of the photograph, scientists can match up the spots to the grid and develop something of a fingerprint of each bear. Dr. Waterman's group has taken more than 10,000 photographs. The whisker spot patterns are so unique they can be used to identify the bears. They watch how polar bears interact with each other and how tourism affects their behavior.

Their special photo-identification software helps her and her team follow individuals. It may help in the future to assess the number of bears that visit the tourist area of Churchill.

Eventually tourists who visit Churchill will be able to help scientists collect data by sending the team their polar bear photos. These photos will allow scientists to identify polar bear individuals visiting the tourist area and see if they come back year after year. This will enable them to come up with an estimate of the number of bears that visit the tourist area each year and to make observations about the weight of the bears.

>> EXPLORER INTERVIEW

DR. STEVEN C. AMSTRUP

BORN: FARGO, NORTH DAKOTA, U.S.A.
JOB TITLE: CHIEF SCIENTIST
AFFILIATION: POLAR BEARS INTERNATIONAL
JOB LOCATIONS: BOZEMAN, MONTANA, U.S.A.; WINNIPEG, MANITOBA, CANADA
YEARS WORKING WITH POLAR BEARS: 34
MONTHS A YEAR IN THE FIELD: EARLY CAREER: 5 MONTHS; TODAY: 2–3 WEEKS

How are you helping to save polar bears?
My research led to the listing of polar bears as a threatened species and illustrated that to save them from extinction we need to dramatically reduce greenhouse-gas emissions. My main function at PBI is to inspire people and policy makers to make necessary changes in time to save polar bears and their sea-ice habitats.

Favorite things about your job?
Polar bears are magical creatures. I love researching them, watching them, and even thinking about them. Most important, I love knowing that there is still time to save them from extinction. If we do that, we will have benefitted the rest of life on Earth. So I think of my job as saving the world one polar bear at a time.

Best thing about working in the field?
The Arctic is a harsh and sometimes scary environment. But on nice days (when it is crisp and cold and sunny), when the leads (openings in the sea ice) are blue and you can see seals and maybe beluga whales swimming there, it is magical.

Worst thing about working in the field?
Although the polar bear's habitat sometimes seems full of life, it is often the other way. When conditions are not right, we have often spent whole days without seeing even one bear. It can be boring, tiring, and frustrating.

How can kids prepare to do your job one day?
Conservation has become very technical. To go into the research side of things, plan on many years in school studying biology, physiology, physics, and math.

>> **MEMORABLE MOMENT**

Polar bears are tough. One year I found two big male polar bears fighting over a female polar bear. One had lost an ear and seemed to have been injured severely in the fight. The other had a 10-inch (25-cm)-long cut in its belly caused in the fight by a tooth or bear claw.

I did not think the bear would survive the deep wound. Yet two years later, I recaptured the same bear.

It was healthy and scrappy. All I could find of that injury was a long scar in the bear's stomach. The fur had grown over it, and I could detect it only by rubbing my fingers over the bear's belly.

Biologist Dr. Steve Amstrup and his assistant, Karyn Rode, use a harness in an attempt to lift a 365-pound (166-kg) female polar bear for further study.

balance the amount of heat energy coming from the sun with the amount transmitted back into space.

However, the overall temperature of Earth is rising. Scientists point to the burning of fossil fuels and deforestation as major causes. These human activities release additional greenhouse gases into the atmosphere, trapping more heat near Earth's surface and warming up the planet.

By the year 2100, Earth's temperature is expected to be three to seven degrees higher than it is now. That may seem like only a small difference, but any slight change can make a big difference on a global scale. Even now we are seeing the effects of this increase in temperature. In 2014 the Carteret Islanders of Papua New Guinea had to leave their island because of rising waters that flooded their crops and threatened their homes. It is predicted that the island will be completely underwater in just a year. They are the first refugees of climate change. Other areas of the world will also flood, including the shorelines of many countries where cities, such as New York, will be affected. To make matters worse, the rise in temperature is speeding up.

These changes have the most impact on the polar regions. Sea ice normally undergoes some melting and refreezing each year, but in recent decades it has been melting more than refreezing. The Arctic ecosystem is out of balance, and animals—from plankton to polar bears—are having a hard time adjusting to the changes.

HELPING HANDS

With more and more sea ice melting, polar bears are forced to search new areas for food, which sometimes pushes them toward people. What happens when a polar bear predator comes to town looking for a bite to eat? Sometimes there is trouble and people have to protect themselves. Installing fences and establishing polar bear patrols can prevent some human and polar bear conflict, but these actions treat the effects rather than the causes. Instead of solving the underlying problem that brings the bears closer to the patrols, they are just reacting to each polar bear conflict.

Fortunately, there are many people across the globe working to help the polar bear population. From scientists studying the bears in the Arctic to school groups combating climate change, the call for help is being heard. You, too, can be part of the action. You can help polar bears wherever you live!

POLAR BEARS IN CAPTIVITY SOMETIMES GROW GREEN ALGAE INSIDE THEIR HOLLOW HAIRS.

Polar bear biologist
Steven Amstrup's tips
for studying polar bears:

1 Learn how to keep yourself—and bears—safe. For example, prepare and secure food away from your camping area.

2 Minimize the impact of your daily activities, or your carbon footprint, to help curb climate change and improve the welfare of polar bears.

3 The study of polar bears involves many fields, from statistics to biology. Find those that are the most interesting to you.

A young bear follows its mother out onto the ice.

>>RESCUE ACTIVITIES

START A CAMPAIGN

A campaign is a series of activities designed to produce a particular result. Starting a campaign is a great way to inform people about the challenges polar bears face and what they can do to help save them. The first and most important part of starting a campaign is to fully understand the problem and what aspects of the solution you want to target. In this challenge, you will learn the basics of starting your very own campaign.

GIVE YOUR CAMPAIGN A NAME

THINK OF A GOOD CAMPAIGN NAME. You could simply use Mission: Polar Bear Rescue, the name of this book, or something else that makes clear what you are trying to do.

MAKE CAMPAIGN STICKERS. Include a logo and slogan, something like "Taking Action for Polar Bears." You could draw your stickers by hand or design them on the computer and print them out.

MAKE T-SHIRTS FOR YOURSELVES. Most stationery shops have fabric pens that you can buy for drawing on your own shirts.

ACT

FORM A TEAM

YOUR CAMPAIGN WILL PROBABLY BE MORE EFFECTIVE and enjoyable if you get a team together. You will benefit from one another's skills and are likely to achieve more.

FOUR IS A GOOD NUMBER OF PEOPLE TO HAVE IN A TEAM. See if you can find three friends who want to help save polar bears. If more people want to get involved, think about having subgroups of four people.

THINK ABOUT YOUR CAMPAIGN OBJECTIVES. Setting goals will help keep everyone on track.

A petition is a letter that asks someone in power to do something. You want to have as many people as possible sign your petition so its message appears to have a lot of support. Here are some tips for writing a good petition:

1 Decide who you are going to send your petition to before you write it. Pick someone who has the power to make a difference, like a politician or business leader.

2 Make clear what the problem is and what you would like them to do about it. The more reasonable your request, the more likely you will be successful.

3 Ask as many people as you can to sign the petition. Posting a petition online is a great way to achieve this, but so is asking your friends or stopping people on the street.

SHARE

Polar Bears, Polar Bear Pictures, Polar Bear Facts - National

SPREAD THE WORD ABOUT YOUR CAMPAIGN

THINK OF ONE ACTION THAT PEOPLE COULD DO TO HELP SAVE POLAR BEARS. You could ask them to sign a petition, do something specific to save energy, or even donate money to a polar bear charity. For starters tell them all about National Geographic's Mission: Animal Rescue initiative!

PUT ON YOUR T-SHIRTS AND GO SOMEWHERE PUBLIC WHERE THERE ARE A LOT OF PEOPLE. Explain to people who pass that you are helping polar bears and ask them to join you in the action you've chosen.

HAND OUT STICKERS. Ask people to wear them somewhere obvicus. The more people who see your stickers, the better!

CHAPTER 2

>> LAND OF POLAR BEARS

"FOR HUMANS, THE ARCTIC IS A HARSHLY INHOSPITABLE PLACE, BUT THE CONDITIONS THERE ARE PRECISELY WHAT POLAR BEARS REQUIRE TO SURVIVE—AND THRIVE."
—SYLVIA EARLE, NATIONAL GEOGRAPHIC EXPLORER-IN-RESIDENCE

Unlike other marine mammals, polar bears spend the majority of their time on ice, not in the water.

Polar bears have sharp claws, thick coats, and powerful jaws full of deadly teeth. But because of their unique Arctic habitat, polar bears have developed some special characteristics that enable them to live at the top of the world.

A DIFFERENT BEAR

Polar bears are one of eight bear species in the Ursidae family. Four species of bear, including the sloth bear, live in southern subtropical forests, while four others, including the polar bear, live in the north. Two species of the northern bears, the brown bear and the polar bear, live in the Arctic.

Perhaps as long as a million years ago, part of the bear population wandered toward the North Pole and eventually adapted to the cold Arctic environment. The Arctic is the region that surrounds the North Pole, which is made up of the Arctic Ocean and the surrounding landmasses—Russia, Greenland, Canada, Norway, Iceland, Sweden, Finland, and the United States. It covers 5.4 million square miles (14 million km^2).

During the summer, the Arctic becomes a land of endless sunshine, but from around Thanksgiving to the end of January, it is plunged into months of

PHYLOGENETIC TREE

Every family has relatives. Some are closer and some more distant. This family tree shows how scientists classify polar bears and their relatives.

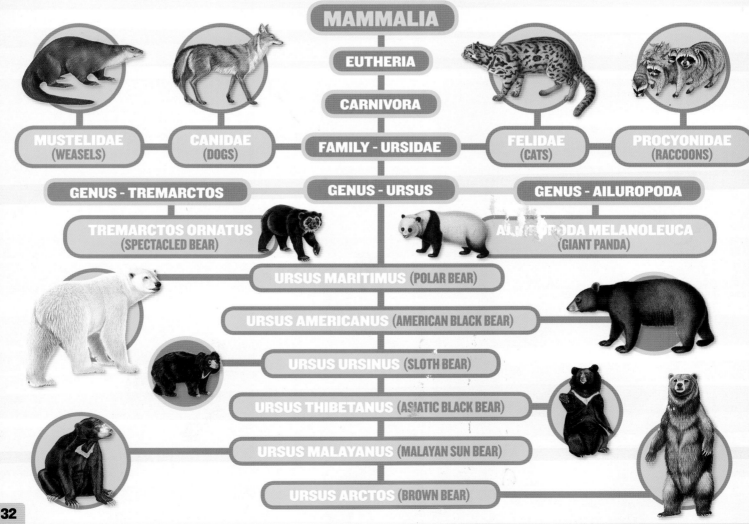

MAMMALIA

EUTHERIA

CARNIVORA

MUSTELIDAE (WEASELS)

CANIDAE (DOGS)

FAMILY - URSIDAE

FELIDAE (CATS)

PROCYONIDAE (RACCOONS)

GENUS - TREMARCTOS

GENUS - URSUS

GENUS - AILUROPODA

TREMARCTOS ORNATUS (SPECTACLED BEAR)

AILUROPODA MELANOLEUCA (GIANT PANDA)

URSUS MARITIMUS (POLAR BEAR)

URSUS AMERICANUS (AMERICAN BLACK BEAR)

URSUS URSINUS (SLOTH BEAR)

URSUS THIBETANUS (ASIATIC BLACK BEAR)

URSUS MALAYANUS (MALAYAN SUN BEAR)

URSUS ARCTOS (BROWN BEAR)

GROLAR AND PIZZLY BEARS

What do you get when a polar bear breeds with a grizzly bear? Scientists call them grolar bears, pizzly bears, or hybrid bears. Sometimes grizzly bears, a species of brown bear, move a little farther north of their territory and polar bears wander a bit farther south, and the two bear species breed together. Their cubs grow up to have a mixture of brown and white fur.

The first recorded wild grolar bear was found near the Beaufort Sea in 2006. The bear was white with patches of brown fur. Scientists tested the animal's DNA to see if it matched with grizzly or polar bear DNA, and genes from both showed up. Since bears often give birth to twins, it would not have been surprising if there were a sibling grolar also in the region.

Another hybrid bear was found in a nearby location in 2010. It looked a lot like a polar bear, but with beige fur. DNA testing showed that it was the cub of a female hybrid bear and a male grizzly bear, which confirmed that grolar bears can reproduce. Perhaps this cub's mom was related to the first grolar found.

Some researchers suspect that as polar bears lose more of their habitat and are forced into areas where grizzlies live, more grolars will appear in the wild.

A mother polar bear calls to her cubs while she rests in the vegetation on the tundra.

SCIENTISTS CAN TEST A BEAR'S BREATH TO DETECT IF IT ATE BERRIES WHILE ON LAND.

Summer in the Arctic brings fields of fireweed and uncomfortably warm temperatures for polar bears.

Polar bear biologist Dr. Thea Bechshoft's tips for studying polar bears:

1 Be patient when watching polar bears, whether in the zoo or in the wild. The more patient you are, the more you'll learn.

2 Get an excellent pair of binoculars and practice using them.

3 Learn all you can about polar bears from books, videos, and by talking to people with polar bear experience.

darkness. Polar bears have adapted to use these light months and dark months as times for resting and times for hunting.

Polar bears have evolved to become some of the biggest bears in the world. A male can stand more than eight feet (2.4 m) tall from head to toe and weigh more than 1,700 pounds (771 kg), although the average bear weighs between 770 and 1,320 pounds (350 and 600 kg). A female is smaller, averaging 330 to 880 pounds (150–400 kg), but can weigh up to about 1,000 pounds (454 kg).

Polar bears spend as little time as possible on land. In fact, some polar bears never come ashore and remain on unmelted ice covering the polar seas throughout the year. But this ice is rapidly disappearing.

POLAR BEAR NEIGHBORHOODS

Today researchers estimate that there are between 20,000 and 25,000 polar bears sharing the Arctic region at the top of the world. They live in different subpopulations, or neighborhoods, that vary in size. Scientists aren't entirely sure why some of these neighborhoods are larger than others.

There are four different ice regions in the Arctic. In one, the ice melts each summer and freezes in the fall. It's tough for polar bears in this region because the seasons have shifted as a result of climate change. The ice melts sooner than usual and freezes later in the fall, leaving less

(continued on p. 41)

POLAR BEARS CAN STORE UP TO HALF OF THEIR BODY WEIGHT AS FAT.

Polar bears can poke their heads through the ice and scan the bottom of shallow bays for food.

SUPER SWIMMERS

Polar bears, often called sea bears, are excellent swimmers.

Polar bears can dive down 15 feet (4.5 m) in the water and stay submerged for more than two minutes.

A polar bear rides an iceberg in Alaska's Beaufort Sea.

Polar bears often break through ice that can't support their weight and swim miles to find ice that can.

EXPLORER INTERVIEW

DR. THEA BECHSHOFT

BORN: DENMARK

JOB TITLE: BIOLOGIST

AFFILIATIONS: UNIVERSITY OF ALBERTA, CANADA; UNIVERSITY OF AARHUS, DENMARK

JOB LOCATIONS: EDMONTON, CANADA; FIELD WORK IN CANADA'S WESTERN HUDSON BAY, MANITOBA, AND VISCOUNT MELVILLE SOUND, NORTHWEST TERRITORIES/NUNAVUT, AND IN SVALBARD, NORWAY, AND EAST GREENLAND.

YEARS WORKING WITH POLAR BEARS: 10

MONTHS A YEAR IN THE FIELD: 2 WEEKS TO 2 MONTHS

How are you helping to save polar bears?
Through my research, I provide a better understanding of how polar bears are doing, especially with regard to their health. The primary focus of my work is studying how the pollution we produce every day affects the polar bears and their chances of survival in a constantly changing environment.

Why are you doing this work?
My greatest aim is to do my part to make sure that polar bears will continue to exist in the wild. I wish for generations and generations of Arctic travelers to be able to experience the privilege that is an encounter with these magnificent creatures in the environment to which they are so perfectly adapted.

The best thing about working in the field?
I love the peace and quiet you often find in the field, along with the spectacular views and wildlife experiences.

How can kids prepare to do your job one day?
Go for walks in nature, observe your pet, read about animals, and be curious about what you see and what you are told. Ask questions—What kind of birds live in your area? How tall can trees get? Where do the insects go in the winter? How do you know whether your dog is happy? Why aren't mice green?—and go looking for answers. A lot of my time is spent reading and writing—practice these skills. Pick up a few useful outdoor skills, too.

>> **MEMORABLE MOMENT**

My first encounter with wild polar bears wasn't with them out in the field: It was in the collection storerooms of the zoological museums in Oslo and Copenhagen. Seeing the line or two identifying the specimens carefully taken down on paper made the bears and their stories come vividly alive to me as I was holding and examining their skulls. It sparked a fascination in me that still holds to this day.

BEAR LINEUP

Check out how the polar bear measures up to its bear cousins!

PANDA
length: 5.5–6 feet (1.7–1.8 m)
weight: 200 pounds (90 kg)

BLACK BEAR
length: 5 feet (1.5 m)
weight: 250–300 pounds (113–136 kg)

POLAR BEAR
length: 8 feet (2.4 meters)
weight: 800–1,600 pounds (363–726 kg)

GRIZZLY, OR BROWN, BEAR
length: 6–7 feet (1.8–2.1 m)
weight: 550 pounds (249 kg)

time for hunting on the ice. Scientists are already seeing decreases in the polar bear population in this area.

The second ice region has sea ice that forms along the shoreline but retreats when the weather gets warm. It takes bears in this region a bit longer to find ice to hunt on these days, meaning they have to use more energy swimming. Even though it is tougher in this area, the polar bear population is not suffering yet. Scientists hope it never will.

The last polar bear neighborhoods are so far north that ice remains year-round. That's a good thing for polar bears. However, if climate change continues, these bears might also have ice problems.

WHAT LIES AHEAD

In 2008, the United States listed polar bears as "threatened" under the Endangered Species Act. Scientists have proved that the temperature of the Earth's atmosphere is rapidly rising. It might be hard to believe when you are experiencing some bitter-cold

TODAY'S SCIENCE, TOMORROW'S SCIENTIST

It is hard to believe that man-made pollution could possibly reach the Arctic, but it has. Dr. Thea Bechshoft is studying the threat of industrial chemicals, like mercury, to bears. Dr. Bechshoft was with her colleagues just outside the small Arctic community of Ittoqqortoormiiit. They were on the sea ice for two to three hours, in minus 4°F (-20°C) or lower, working intensely and under time pressure to get organ samples for pollution research from a polar bear brought in by one of the local hunters as part of their legal yearly quota.

The whole town joined the group to see what was happening, but Dr. Bechshoft especially remembered one boy who stood next to her the entire time, asking question after question. She was more than happy to answer the best she could with all that was going on—sharp knives, howling dogs, crowds of people, and a polar bear mother and her two cubs closing in on them. Finally, she told the shivering boy with lips that were slowly turning blue to go home, which he begrudgingly did.

The next day she met the boy's mother, who said all her son talked about since they had met on the ice was how he wanted to become a biologist. Dr. Bechshoft's work is not only helping today's Arctic polar bears, it is also setting the stage for tomorrow's scientists. With her help polar bears will go on being studied—and saved!

days, but scientists point to climate, not day-to-day weather patterns, to assess the warming of our planet. Many scientists believe that climate change is creating the extreme weather patterns we are experiencing all over the world.

As the planet's temperature increases, the ice in the Arctic Circle melts, leaving dark, open ocean water that absorbs more heat from the sun than reflective ice. That causes the Arctic to experience a warming about twice the global average. The melting ice disrupts the ecosystem, making it difficult for polar bears to find food.

In addition to climate change, further threats include oil drilling, road construction, and hunting. Also, harmful chemicals are poisoning the Arctic food web because of pollution carried on ocean currents from around the world. Even though polar bears live in a distant land, the choices we make every day are affecting their future. If we can save the Arctic, we can save polar bears and everything that depends on the frozen north.

The Trans-Alaska oil pipeline cuts through more than 800 miles (1,287 km) of polar bear territory to transport oil from Prudhoe Bay to Valdez, Alaska.

THE OLDEST WILD POLAR BEAR EVER RECORDED WAS 32 YEARS OLD.

A polar bear walks on ice in the northeastern Svalbard archipelago. Norway aims to make this region one of the most preserved wilderness areas in the world.

>> RESCUE ACTIVITIES

BE A POLAR EXPLORER

Polar bears are incredible polar explorers. They have to be in order to find food and survive. Bears will walk 20 miles (32 km) in a day searching for a meal. A healthy bear can swim over 200 miles (322 km) in a single swim, with one recorded swimming over 400 miles (644 km).

As ice melts, many polar bears are being forced to swim longer distances to survive. This is especially bad news for young cubs that find it harder to swim.

This rescue challenge shows how you can raise money or awareness for a charity by getting out and thinking like a polar bear!

MAKE

MAKE A PLAN TO RAISE MONEY FOR A POLAR BEAR CHARITY OR MISSION: ANIMAL RESCUE. *You could:*

ASK FRIENDS and family to give you a donation for a charity that helps polar bears.

HOLD A POLAR BEAR SOFT-TOY CENSUS in your school. Suggest that everyone who has a cuddly polar bear toy should donate one dollar in return for the comfort it gives them.

GET SPONSORED to walk, swim, bike, dance, skate, or take part in some other kind of activity. Do something impressive and you are likely to collect more money.

ORGANIZE AN EVENT that other people can get involved with. If you have lots of people being sponsored to do an activity you will raise even more funds and support for the charity.

ACT

TAKE ACTION BY:

SLIDING LIKE A POLAR BEAR ON ICE. Organize a competition on an ice rink or on a Slip 'N Slide to see who can go the farthest.

WALKING 20 MILES (32 KM), the distance a polar bear would walk in a typical day. This is a serious challenge, so consider doing the walk over two or even three days.

SWIMMING 426 MILES (686 KM), the longest recorded distance that a polar bear has managed to swim. Doing this on your own will be very hard, but could you persuade 426 people to swim one mile (1.6 km) each?

SHARE

CELEBRATE YOUR SUCCESS!

HAVE A SMALL PARTY TO CELEBRATE YOUR SUCCESS. Be sure to give a short speech and thank everyone who took part, even if it is just three of you!

AT YOUR EVENT, GIVE PEOPLE CARDS OR BROCHURES that explain the problems polar bears are facing and how they can help. Ask people to share photos from the event online.

LET YOUR LOCAL MEDIA KNOW WHAT YOU HAVE ACHIEVED and ask them to write a story about it. Be prepared to answer questions about why you organized the event. They might want some photos, too.

Raising money for polar bear charities is one of the most effective things you can do to help. Here are some top tips for fund-raising:

1 Read this entire book before you start fund-raising. You will know an incredible amount about polar bears and will be better equipped to answer people's questions.

2 Pick your polar bear charity carefully. Before giving money, many people will want to know exactly how their investment will be spent.

3 Persuade a local business to match whatever you raise. This means they will donate the same amount that you fund-raise to your named charity.

CHAPTER 3

>> LIFE BEGINS ON THE ICE

"POLAR BEARS ARE CREATURES OF THE SEA ICE. IF IT DISAPPEARS, SO WILL THEY."

—KIERAN MULVANEY, AUTHOR OF *THE GREAT WHITE BEAR*

Even though they spend most of
their time on the ice, polar bears
are powerful swimmers.

After three dark months of winter, a new year begins each February in the Arctic. But that doesn't mean those days of winter were quiet. While the wind howled and blew across the icy landscape, just feet below the snowy surface mother polar bears were giving birth.

CUBS ARE BORN

Polar bear cubs, weighing just about a pound (0.5 kg), are born with almost no hair covering their small, pink bodies. They measure about 12 to 14 inches (30–35 cm) long and spend their early days crawling through their mother's thick fur to nurse at her belly. The hungry youngsters latch on and make humming sounds as they drink her warm milk.

POLAR BEARS GROW TO 30 TIMES THEIR BIRTH WEIGHT BY THE TIME THEY ARE READY TO LEAVE THE DEN.

Mother polar bears give birth to their young between the months of November and February and remain in the den until spring.

A three-month-old cub nuzzles in its mother's thick warm fur.

Polar bears do not hibernate like other bears, but mother bears do enter dens to give birth. The demands of pregnancy, birth, and nursing their young create a need for the bears to maintain a higher body temperature during this time. They spend months in their winter dens without daylight or food. They live off the layer of fat built up by eating seals last spring. Their bodies enable them to recycle their waste so they can live for months in the den without urinating.

The dens are dug into snowdrifts in the fall. Although dark, the cozy den is 40 degrees warmer than the frigid Arctic winter air outside.

As the winter ends, the mother bears leave their dens to travel back to the sea ice to eat again. The cubs will follow for the first time into the frozen world.

ON THE MOVE

On a sunny day in late February, mother bears break through the snow covering their dens. They poke their black noses into the air and sniff. When they feel it is safe to emerge, they squeeze their huge bodies out of the small openings.

The mother bears stand guard while their cubs scamper in the snow. Mother bears emerge from their dens hungry. They have been without food all winter, and nursing the newborns has drawn down their fat reserves. They cannot stay near their dens for long because they need to eat, and the only food is located on the sea ice a few miles away.

THE JOURNEY BEGINS

Mother bears and cubs leave the den behind. The cubs, called coy their first year, begin their lifelong journey in search of food on the sea ice.

Early spring still carries winter's chill, and the temperature can drop to minus 40°F (-40°C). A mother bear emerges in a state similar to a denning black bear, but her body temperature is a few degrees

>> **SPOTLIGHT**
SEA ICE

Not all ice is the same. Here are five different types of ice that are found in the Arctic.

Pressure ridges: stretches of ice chunks that pile up when large pieces of ice collide

Pack ice: offshore moving ice that varies in thickness and character

TO HELP OR NOT TO HELP

Scientists are always put into difficult situations when they see an animal in distress. They must decide whether they should intervene or let nature take its course and perhaps lose the animal.

That happened to Dr. Nikita Ovsyanikov in the autumn of 2003 at Russia's Wrangel Island. He spotted a couple of that year's orphan cubs, running around without their mother. He couldn't know what had happened to them and why they were orphaned.

"That was an ice-free season and there were many polar bears stranded onshore at Wrangel Island then," he says.

The two orphan cubs were among them. One of them did not survive the autumn, but the other managed to survive until the ocean started freezing. Dr. Ovsyanikov knew the cub would not survive the harsh winter.

"Normally I never interfere with polar bear life, just observe whatever happens. In this case I decided to give her some food, to make her be a bit happier in her first and last autumn."

He gave her a reindeer carcass and observed her eating it during the night. The next day he found her sleeping on new ice that was blown away into the open sea. That was the last he saw of her that fall.

But the next autumn Dr. Ovsyanikov returned to continue his research. There were again many bears around.

"To my greatest surprise," he says, "my small female came back, one year older and in good health! I recognized her by appearance and behavior."

The bear came straight to him. "No one other bear would behave this way." It is unusual that orphan cubs could survive alone their first winter.

The decision to provide the cub food helped her survive before she went to scavenge on the sea ice that winter. Sometimes a simple act can mean the difference between life and death, but the question of when and if to act is never simple.

Pancake ice: circular pieces of ice that form in rough waters and are tricky to navigate

Frazil: needle-like crystals that gather on the sea surface when it starts to freeze

Nilas: a thin, flexible sheet of newly formed ice

MARATHON SWIMMER

Polar bears can swim hundreds of miles, but news of a female swimming for over 400 miles (687 km) was unheard of. According to researchers at the U.S. Geological Survey, the bear they tracked, polar bear 20741, swam for about nine days—232 hours in water just above freezing. That's like swimming from Boston to Washington, D.C.!

When the bear was located again on land in Alaska, she had lost 22 percent of her body weight, a lot for a polar bear. Scientists are pointing to a lack of sea ice for these long swims. This polar bear mother was strong enough for the long journey, but her cub was not able to make it with her.

higher. The cubs have grown over the winter, from about a pound (0.5 kg) to between 22 and 33 pounds (10–15 kg). They'll weigh close to 100 pounds (45 kg) by their eighth month. Their mother's milk is 31 percent fat. Even though they will begin their hunting lessons on the ice, they will continue to nurse from their mother for their first two years.

The mother bears hunt for ringed seals. Seals have their pups in shallow caves dug in snowdrifts on the ice. Polar bears rely on seals for their fat, or blubber, which keeps them warm while swimming in the Arctic waters. But because of climate change, the window of time before weather warms up and the sea ice begins to melt is getting progressively shorter. No ice means polar bears don't have access to seals, and in some areas, polar bears are suffering from too short a time on the ice.

LIFE ON THE ICE

The springtime ice creaks beneath a full-grown polar bear's weight. Once the mother bear catches a whiff of a seal, she will rise up on her hind legs. Boom, boom! The female bear, just like a hunting male, will pounce down hard with her front paws, trying to punch through the hard-packed snow into the seal lair, where seals raise their young. Young cubs watch their mother and start to imitate her. They are learning to hunt.

The mother bear breaks through and plunges head-first into the den, coming up with a seal pup in her jaws—food at last.

During the winter, an average mother polar bear could lose 300 pounds (136 kg), leaving her a skinny 400 pounds (181 kg). She needs to eat a lot of seals to build up that weight again.

(continued on p. 57)

>> ANIMAL RESCUE!

SAVING ORPHANS

Operation Snowflake began in early 2011 when oil workers in Alaska spotted a cub that had been separated from its mother. They called the U.S. Fish and Wildlife Service, or USFWS, which found the cub near Alaska's North Slope and rescued her from certain death.

The infant had previously been monitored with its sibling and mother in February, but the mother's radio collar had come off and the scientists lost track of the group. In April the cub was spotted alone.

After two months in the care of the Alaska Zoo, Qannik—or "snowflake" in the Iñupiat language—moved to a permanent home at the Louisville Zoo in Kentucky.

In March 2013, the USFWS and Alaska Zoo rescued another polar bear cub, whose mother was shot by a hunter near Point Lay, Alaska. The baby bear was named Kali and was moved to New York to live with another cub named Luna, who had been abandoned by her mother.

Since human hands raised the orphaned cubs, they have not learned to hunt seals. Without learning their mothers' hunting skills, they would not survive on their own. Instead

they have become Arctic ambassadors, creating a link between zoogoers and the sea ice at the top of the world. The hope is that as people watch these polar bears, they will also learn about the hardships wild bears face as climate change continues to alter the Arctic habitat.

>> EXPLORER INTERVIEW

DR. NIKITA OVSYANIKOV

BORN: VIENNA, AUSTRIA
JOB: SENIOR RESEARCH SCIENTIST
JOB LOCATION: WRANGEL ISLAND STATE NATURE RESERVE, RUSSIA
YEARS WORKED IN THE ARCTIC REGION? 24
MONTHS IN THE FIELD: 3 TO 4 MONTHS

How are you helping to save polar bears?
By doing field research on the polar bear population and behavioral ecology we are gaining knowledge that is essential for understanding the rules of their life, the problems they are facing, the actual threats, and what factors are important for them to survive in the changing world. Sharing this knowledge makes more people aware of the problem. The next step is to influence decisions that are critical for polar bear conservation. I also teach people to respect and protect polar bears.

Favorite thing about your job?
When our teams succeeded in keeping the ban on polar bear hunting in Russia.

Best thing about working in the field?
The feeling of freedom and the enjoyment of nature's beauty. I love witnessing the drama of the animals' everyday life.

Worst thing about working in the field?
The separation from your loved ones, if they cannot be with you!

How can kids prepare to do your job one day?
Be healthy. Be rather universal in your skills. Learn about animals and nature in advance as much as you can. Respect animals and Mother Nature. Get a good education as a zoologist—this is important not only for the field work, but also as a basic education for understanding the world, the value of life, the nature of animals and humans, and for broadening your mind. It is also important for realizing our responsibility for the life on our planet in all its forms.

A polar bear cub pokes its head out of its den after a long winter in Hudson Bay, Canada.

AN EXPECTANT POLAR BEAR WILL DIG MANY DEN HOLES UNTIL SHE SETTLES ON THE RIGHT SPOT TO REMAIN DURING HER WINTER PREGNANCY.

MOST POLAR BEARS GIVE BIRTH TO TWINS.

>> **EXPERT TIPS**

Senior research scientist Dr. Nikita Ovsyanikov's tips for studying polar bears:

1 Respect polar bears! Truly honor their freedom and right to live in their environment.

2 Remember that bears are predators and can be dangerous. It is important to make sure that everyone, including the bears, is safe.

3 Do not harm or disturb animals. You gather the most objective information about animals when you observe them in their natural state.

One 20-pound (9-kg) ringed seal pup is a small meal to share between three mouths, but it is just the start of hunting season. Cubs learn how to clean their fur after eating by watching their mother roll in the snow.

HOMELESS BOUND?

Finding a good spot for a den is important for a polar bear that is going to have cubs. Most polar bears den on land, but there are some that make dens on moving ice floes. About half of the bears studied near Alaska den on the sea ice. Dens on the ice are far from human activities like drilling for oil and mining, which can disturb the bears in the den. The downside is that sea ice can crack and destroy the den without any warning. Plus, a floating ice platform could carry the family hundreds of miles from where it began. When the bears emerge in the spring, they hope to step out to a seal cornucopia, but there is no guarantee.

These days, researchers are finding more land based dens in Alaska, most likely because the sea ice is melting and is not very stable. A mother bear does not want to take the risk of falling through the ice with newborns, so if she thinks the ice is too thin,

she will den on land. If ice stretches all the way to the shore, she can den on the ice close to shore, so that she can exit her den on solid ground when the ice begins to melt. Ice-free water can prevent mother bears from reaching shore in fall. Researchers in Svalbard, Norway, have shown a direct relationship between when the ice freezes and the numbers of females reaching traditional denning areas. They are watching the bears closely to see how climate change will affect their ability to go into dens and have cubs in the future.

>> POLAR BEAR SPOTLIGHT
STAYING COOL

During the hottest summer months of June through September, polar bears could overheat if they don't find ways to cool down.

A nice dip in the ocean usually works.

Finding a shady spot to rest can help.

Digging a pit into the snow will cool a bear right down.

SNIFFER DOG DETECTS

Dogs have an amazing sense of smell. Many are employed in search-and-rescue and detection work and helping conservationists. A beagle named Elvis has put his nose to work to sniff out polar bear pregnancies at the Cincinnati Zoo. Elvis has been trained to sniff polar bear feces, or poop, to detect which samples are from pregnant females. Specifically, the dog has been sniffing out Berit, the zoo's female who has displayed pregnancy symptoms. Berit didn't turn out to be pregnant this time around, but hopefully in the future the zoo will welcome a pair of polar bear cubs. Elvis will be on hand to help!

ACTIONS SPEAK LOUDER THAN WORDS

Polar bears are in trouble, but there are things you can do to help them.

Polar bears have adapted to live in the very cold Arctic, but this region is slowly heating up. The warming is caused, in part, by the fuels we burn in vehicles and used to run our homes and factories.

Most climate change scientists agree that we need to use less of these harmful fuels to reduce the damage we are doing to polar bear habitats. This activity will show you how you can do your part right away.

FOOD & WATER

MAKE SOME CHANGES

FOOD. When cooking, make sure you use lids on pans. Less energy will be needed to heat up your food and keep it warm.

WATER. Avoid buying bottled water. As well as being more expensive than tap water, far more energy is used in getting it to you. Instead, fill a refillable bottle with your own water before you leave home.

EFFICIENCY. Energy is needed to make water clean and move it around. Spending less time showering and running water are just two ways you can help save energy.

ENERGY

CHANGE YOUR DAILY ROUTINE

CHILL OUT. Turn your heat down by one degree in the winter. If you have air conditioning, turn it up by one degree in the summer.

SWITCH OFF. Turn lights and appliances off when you are not using them.

GET OUTSIDE. The more time you spend in the outdoors, the less energy you'll use on the TV, lights, and more!

TRAVEL

DO MORE TOGETHER

SHARE A JOURNEY. Public transportation is usually better for the environment than traveling in a private car, so use a shared bus or train when you can.

SHARE A WALK. Walk or bike instead of riding in a car whenever you can. Take a look at a map and see what places are just one mile (1.6 km) away. It will only take you about 20 minutes to walk that distance and will save burning fuel.

EAT LOCAL FOOD. It takes lots of energy to transport food. Buying food that has been grown locally will help reduce your energy use.

>> **EXPERT TIPS**

You will need to persuade parents, teachers, or other adults to let you take action to reduce how much energy you use. Here are some good arguments you can use to help your cause:

1 Using less energy is good for the environment. It not only helps to tackle climate change, but pollution too.

2 Using less energy will save your family money. Why not use the money for a vacation or a weekend activity?

3 Walking or riding a bicycle not only uses less energy, but it also keeps you fit and healthy.

CHAPTER 4

>>>ICE HUNTERS

"THIS PLACE IS LIKE SUSHI FOR BEARS."

—ERIC McNAIR-LANDRY, NATIONAL GEOGRAPHIC YOUNG EXPLORER

A polar bear feeds on a freshly caught seal on a small Arctic ice floe.

Polar bears are fierce predators. Life in this cold habitat requires lots of energy and fat to stay warm and to move their big bodies. Bears need to be master hunters. They must be patient and fast to capture seals. They must be strong and powerful to avoid painful walrus tusks.

Some say the people of the Arctic have developed hunting skills from observing the great bears in action.

TOP OF THE FOOD CHAIN

Polar bears top the who-eats-who food chain in the Arctic. They are fourth-level consumers, meaning they prey on third-level consumers, seals. The seal is itself a predator that preys on creatures that are also predators. Seals consume fish and shellfish. Aside from humans and some whales, polar bears reign supreme

Waiting for a seal to emerge from the water is a test of patience for hungry polar bears.

POLAR BEARS CAN MAKE THEIR OWN WATER, CALLED METABOLIC WATER, WHEN THEY DIGEST SEAL FAT.

A polar bear drags a young bearded seal across an ice pack in Norway.

among the global food chains. Even wolves are considered lower food-chain predators because they prey on creatures that feed only on organic material.

Only skilled hunters survive in the harsh Arctic landscape. Polar bears have an incredible sense of smell that allows them to sniff out a seal three feet (1 m) under the ice. But only 1 in 20 hunts is successful.

SUCCESSFUL HUNTERS

To be successful hunters in the snowy environment, polar bears evolved white fur for camouflage. Most bears eat plants, berries, and fish, but polar bears adapted to the Arctic climate by eating seals—specifically, seal blubber. Seal blubber is the perfect food. A good-size seal can provide a polar bear with about eight days' worth of energy. It is loaded with calories. The seal provides twice as much energy as a steak dinner. Polar bears will also

ON AVERAGE, ONE POLAR BEAR NEEDS TO CATCH 43 RINGED SEALS A YEAR JUST TO SURVIVE.

occasionally hunt walruses that can weigh 1,300 to 2,200 pounds (600–1,000 kg) for a male, as well as a heavy beluga whale.

Polar bears wait patiently for seals to come up for air. They know from their sense of smell and from the disruption of water in the seal's breathing hole in the ice that one will eventually surface. But seals have numerous holes to choose from and might not surface at that hole for a long while. The bear waits. Sooner or later the seal may return and, if so, the bear will grab it. Most hunts, however, are unsuccessful.

Polar bears rely on the sea ice forming each year to give them access to seals. Hunting is most successful when they sit on the ice platforms over shallow waters closest to shore.

Polar bears will also search out seals in the late

(continued on p. 71)

ANIMAL SUPERPOWERS

CONSERVING ENERGY

POLAR BEARS NEED TO CONSERVE ENERGY DURING LEAN TIMES.

WALKING SLOWLY SAVES ENERGY.

CURLING UP TO STAY WARM DURING A BLIZZARD IS A PRIME ENERGY SAVER.

POLAR BEARS ALSO SAVE ENERGY BY LOWERING THEIR METABOLIC RATE AND ENTERING A STATE CALLED WALKING HIBERNATION.

POLAR BEAR WHISPERER MATTHAIS BREITER <<<

Biologist, author, and photographer Matthais Breiter aims to increase the understanding and acceptance of polar bears through his work and experiences in the Arctic.

"Stereotypes such as 'polar bears are the only carnivore that hunt humans' and 'bears including polar bears are unpredictable, solitary, and in essence asocial' are commonly accepted as fact. Both statements or assumptions are wrong, but their widespread acceptance as truth results in many bears being shot in defense of life and property," says Breiter.

He spends several months each year with polar bears and has never had to use anything but body language to work with the animals. He's never had to shoot an animal or even use cracker shells—which make very loud noises when thrown at the ground—to discourage their approach. He finds polar bears quite social and reasonably easy to work with on the ground.

Breiter attempts to work solely as an observer in the Arctic, without interfering with the animals in any manner. "However, sometimes the mere presence of a person can be used by the animals in their interaction with each other," he says.

Breiter has observed the hierarchy that develops among the polar bears when, for example, they congregate around a large food source, such as a whale carcass. Using his own body language to show dominance, he has been able to prevent larger curious males from approaching too close. Soon, juvenile polar bears and females with cubs realize that a male-free buffer zone exists around him. Under these circumstances, Breiter has observed that the juveniles use him as a shield from large adult animals, even sleeping behind him.

Females with cubs have also used him for protection. Once, a female with cubs spotted him from over a mile away and ran toward him, her cubs in tow. She stopped about 30 yards (27 m) short. Breiter saw that a wolf had been tracking her. The female was using Breiter as protection, shielding her cubs from the wolf, a dangerous threat to them. The wolf eventually wandered off.

>> EXPLORER INTERVIEW

SARAH McNAIR-LANDRY

BORN: THUNDER BAY, CANADA
JOB: ADVENTURER, CINEMATOGRAPHER, AND POLAR GUIDE
JOB LOCATION: GOBI, NORTH POLE, SOUTH POLE, GREENLAND
YEARS WORKED IN THE ARCTIC REGION: 10

How are you helping to save polar bears?
Through my expeditions I want to inspire young people to get outside and to be active, promoting a healthy lifestyle and a respect for the environment. Also, I educate other polar explorers in how to respect and interact with polar bears without harming them.

Favorite thing about your job?
I get to be outside for months at a time.

Best thing about working in the field?
I get to discover amazing remote places where very few people get to travel. These expeditions have also led me to interesting situations, like ending up face-to-face with a polar bear.

Worst thing about working in the field?
Often on expeditions, I end up in difficult situations and environments. There are days when it's tough traveling conditions and so cold that I wish I could be home in a warm bed.

How can kids prepare to do your job one day?
Get outside and get active! Start by camping on your back porch. Then head out for an overnight trip. This is the best way to practice camping skills. As you become more experienced, head out into the wilderness for longer and longer trips.

Halfway through an 85-day kite-skiing expedition across the Northwest Passage, we were awakened by something brushing up against our tent wall. Seconds later, a polar bear's front paws were crushing the tent, landing on my chest. Out of my sleeping bag in seconds, I screamed and kicked at the tent wall.

It took a lot of yelling, setting off a flare, and firing a warning shot over the bear's head to scare it off. During the next 12 hours, my brother and I saw another five bears. Intimidated by the attack, it took weeks before we could sleep soundly.

Sarah McNair-Landry hauling gear over the rough Arctic terrain

>> ANIMAL RESCUE!

<<<

GARBAGE PICKERS

For decades, the promise of leftovers lured polar bears to a garbage dump in the town of Churchill in Canada. Hungry bears picked through piles of trash and feasted on the scraps humans left behind.

Mother bears made garbage picking a survival technique and brought their cubs here to wait out the ice-free months when they could not hunt seals. Researchers captured and marked each polar bear that came to the dump so they could keep track of their comings and goings. One bear was tagged for 18 years! But these garbage bears were not clean and white—their coats were dirty and dingy, and they had large numbers spray-painted on their fur for easy tracking.

Problems arose when the polar bears wandered into town. They would break into houses looking for food, so the local conservation group trapped and relocated the more aggressive bears. Even then, there was no guarantee the bears would stay away. When the dump finally closed, the bears had to adjust to life without handouts, but now everyone—the bears and the people—is safer.

Ringed seals, averaging 150 pounds (68 kg) each, live throughout polar bear territory. Seal pups, found in ice lairs, are about 40 pounds (18 kg) in the spring.

>> POLAR BEAR SPOTLIGHT
POLAR BEAR PREY

Polar bears hunt on the ice. These species top their food list.

Harp seals, averaging 285 pounds (129 kg), are found in the North Atlantic and lower Arctic waters.

winter when their breathing holes are covered with snow. In late winter and spring, ringed seals will carve a cave out of the snow that has fallen on the ice, if it is deep enough, to give birth to their pups. Polar bears can detect these spots. They will rise up on hind legs and pounce down, crashing through the chamber to grab a bite.

THE SUMMER FAST

Polar bears can survive without eating for months if they have stored lots of fat on their bodies. Some bears do this every summer they spend on land.

Trouble happens when the ice melts too early and the frozen white blanket shrinks toward the North Pole. When the ice melts farther and farther from shore, as it has in Alaska, it is no longer good for seal hunting. Seals can survive in the shallow waters

Walruses—with weights of 1,800 to 3,000 pounds (816–1,361 kg)—can be found in the Chukchi Sea, northeast Canada, and West Greenland.

Beluga whales, weighing 3,300 pounds (1,497 kg), sometimes get trapped in sea-ice openings.

Bearded seals, averaging 575 to 800 pounds (260–360 kg), are the largest species of Arctic seal inhabiting the Arctic Ocean.

SWIMMING GUS

Many city zoos now have resident polar bears, including New York City's. Gus came to the city from the Toledo Zoo in 1988 and quickly gained the affection of zoo visitors who came to see him at the Central Park Zoo. But in 1994, Gus began to swim lap after lap in his pool in figure-eight patterns for as many as 12 hours a day, 7 days a week. Although visitors flocked to see the swimming polar bear, zoo officials worried about his behavior.

They studied Gus's appetite and other behaviors to see if there was a problem with him. People thought he was a bit crazy, and his odd behavior spawned a play, *Gus,* and a book, *What's Worrying Gus? The True Story of a Big City Bear.* A professional animal behaviorist was brought in to examine Gus. He found that Gus simply was bored.

Zookeepers began an enrichment program for Gus that included special polar bear "toys" like mackerel frozen in ice, chicken wrapped in rawhide, and rubber garbage cans to keep him busy and happy.

His swimming decreased, but it never went away entirely. After all, polar bears do like to swim!

throughout the summer, but the polar bears can't catch the seals in open water. They need the platforms the ice creates, and fewer seals are found where the ice remains.

Adult polar bears are good swimmers—some can go for hundreds of miles. But long-distance swimming means there's no ice, and swimming requires a lot more energy than walking, especially if a storm blows in. Researchers and native hunters have seen dead adult polar bears that have drowned in open water. Scientists report that climate change is melting the sea ice faster and faster, which would result in polar bears needing to swim longer distances to find food and having less time to hunt. Nobody knows how polar bears will adapt to their changing habitat— or if they will be able to at all.

SCAVENGER POLAR BEARS

Over the last 30 years, the spring thaw has ended earlier and the autumn has frozen later. Polar bears have had to spend nearly a month longer on land than they used to. More time on land means hungrier bears. Some polar bears are dealing with the loss by seeking out other food sources, including bird eggs. Although some individual polar bears may benefit from eating lots of eggs, whether a large number of bears would benefit is unclear. What is clear is that bird populations may suffer if the bears repeatedly eat their eggs.

Eggs are not the only extra food source for opportunistic polar bears. Sometimes large whales, narwhals, and walruses get trapped in a small opening in the pack ice, called savsatt. They become easy prey for waiting polar bears. Scientists once observed about 100 polar bears feasting on the body of a dead gray whale! This was not the only group banquet on record. In another encounter, 14 bears were seen eating a walrus carcass side by side. Polar bears will share a carcass with another bear if that bear has arrived low to the ground in a submissive approach. This is followed by a slow circle around the desired meal and a respectful touch on the nose of the dominant, in-charge polar bear.

Polar bears may not be picky eaters, but their main sources of food are still the animals they hunt, and they should be. All of their food sources rely on a healthy Arctic environment. Without a healthy environment, animal diversity is lost, and the polar bears will be as well.

Polar bears, like these eating a whale carcass, are excellent scavengers and have even been known to share their finds with other bears.

POLAR BEAR BODY LANGUAGE

If you ever meet a polar bear in the wild, it is good to know what it might be feeling. Here are some hints.

A polar bear will flatten her ears and turn away from whatever she finds annoying.

If he feels threatened, a polar bear might stomp his feet or charge.

A yawning bear might not be tired. He might be stressed out.

>>RESCUE ACTIVITIES

WRITE A POLAR BEAR COOKBOOK

This challenge is about creating a polar bear–friendly cookbook—not cooking up polar bears!

If we all ate exactly like polar bears, the planet would be in trouble! Polar bears are carnivores, and if every human ate as much meat as a polar bear, it would not be good for the environment. To feed the human population, we've created farms, where lots of animals are kept together. Though convenient food sources, the world's 59 billion farm animals are responsible for an estimated 37 percent of the methane in the atmosphere. Scientists believe this gas contributes to climate change even more than carbon dioxide.

Eating less meat is a major thing that you can do to reduce your impact on climate change.

MAKE A SCRAPBOOK

of environmentally friendly recipes and cooking techniques. You will need an adult to help you with this challenge.

SHOP FOR LOCALLY PRODUCED FOODS that are healthy and do not require transport over a long distance.

FIND FOODS THAT HAVE BEEN MINIMALLY PROCESSED. Heavily processed and packaged foods use up far more energy than others. Growing fruit and vegetables in a garden yourself is a great way to get environmentally friendly food, too!

COLLECT MEAT FREE RECIPES. Animals make methane, and they take a lot of energy to rear. Dining on plants, especially local ones, is often the most environmentally friendly way to eat.

SAVE ENERGY. EAT IN THE DARK!

POLAR BEAR COOK BOOK

ACT

WRITE A SHORT POLAR BEAR COOKBOOK OF RECIPES THAT HELP TACKLE CLIMATE CHANGE

TEST AFFORDABLE RECIPES that use as little energy as possible to prepare and cook. Make improvements to them until they are very tasty.

THERE ARE MANY GREAT WAYS TO SHARE YOUR POLAR BEAR COOKBOOK

COOK A MEAL FROM YOUR BOOK for friends and family. You will be able to use the meal to explain what your polar bear cookbook is and why it is important.

GIVE A COPY OF YOUR COOKBOOK to the cafeteria at your school. Challenge them to make a polar bear recipe that will use less energy in the school kitchens.

PUBLISH YOUR COOKBOOK. You could print copies, make it available to download as an ebook, or start blogging recipes on the Internet. The more people who try your recipes, the better.

TAKE PHOTOS OF YOUR DISHES to go alongside your recipes. Be careful to get your food into focus and make it look delicious.

WRITE EACH RECIPE INTO YOUR BOOK. Make sure you give a clear list of ingredients, guidance on how to find them, and step-by-step cooking instructions.

Here are some great ways to use less energy when making food:

1
Growing your own food is easier than you might think. Ask your local hardware store or garden shop for some advice on the best fruits and vegetables to grow.

2
Cooking more food than you need wastes time, energy, money, and ingredients, so make sure to plan and portion your meals carefully.

3
Eat foods that you don't have to cook, such as veggies. Research delicious and nutritious meals you can make without having to burn any fuel.

CHAPTER 5

>>> POLAR BEARS AND PEOPLE

" MANY PEOPLE FIND SOMETHING MYSTICAL ABOUT A HUGE, POTENTIALLY DANGEROUS, PURE WHITE PREDATOR THAT STAYS AWAKE ALL WINTER, WALKING ON A FROZEN OCEAN UNDER THE NORTHERN LIGHTS. "

—ANDREW DEROCHER, POLAR BEAR BIOLOGIST

Expeditions to see polar bears in the wild have become increasingly popular, especially in Hudson Bay.

Polar bears and people have a long history together in the Arctic, dating back to early cave paintings found in the Chukchi Peninsula of Siberia. Remains of polar bears have been located in primitive hunting sites dating from 2,500 to 3,000 years ago. Over many years, our relationship with the bears has been tested. We have now reached a time when protecting the bears is crucial to our own future.

LIVING WITH POLAR BEARS

About four million people currently live above the boundary of the Arctic Circle—in the land of the polar bear. Most live in cities in Canada, Russia, and Norway that

A curious polar bear smells food and peeks through an open window in Churchill, Manitoba, Canada.

POLAR BEAR PATROL

The phone rings just before midnight at Brett Wlock's place in Churchill, Canada. Someone has spotted a curious polar bear wandering around town. Churchill has become a mecca for people wanting to view polar bears.

Wlock is a natural-resources officer with the Manitoba Conservation and Water Stewardship Agency. His job is to keep Churchill safe from the hundreds of polar bears that come ashore each summer. Wlock and his team locate the intruder within two minutes. Using a truck with a siren, they convince the bear to leave town. Nobody, including the bear, is hurt in the process.

Churchill may be a popular ecotourism site for humans, but it is like a roadside attraction for traveling polar bears. They are hungry and curious, and they can harm people and property if not handled properly. Wlock says they first try to wrangle a polar bear out of town with a truck, and if that doesn't work they will shoot loud cracker shells to scare it away. Any repeat offenders are rounded up with a cage trap and placed in what the locals call "polar bear jail."

Inside, each holding cell is about the size of a one-car garage. Wlock says the bears stay locked up for about 30 days. When it is moving time, Wlock drugs the bears so they sleep. Each bear gets examined and tagged with a number, which helps researchers keep track of a bear's health and history. Then the bear is carried to a net that hangs from a helicopter. The chopper airlifts the polar bears about 75 miles (121 km) north of Churchill.

<<<

A wandering polar bear is lifted away from town by a helicopter. The bear will be transported to a safe area, away from people.

Hunting quotas allow the Inuit people to hunt a limited number of polar bears.

began as shipping and hunting ports, military posts, and mining towns. Others make up indigenous communities.

Polar bears make appearances all over the coasts surrounding the North Pole, so people have stories, pictures, and videos of curious polar bears wandering into town and occasionally causing trouble as they look for food.

In communities where polar bears tend to visit often, the town will have a polar bear patrol unit to protect both people and the animals from each other. In most cases the unwelcome guests are shooed away with loud cracker shells and rubber bullets before they do any real harm to people and property. If a polar bear is a return visitor, patrollers may have to relocate it many miles away.

Many of the Inuit, Inuvialuit, Inupiat, Yup'iit, and Chukchi people living along the northern coasts of the Arctic rely on hunting marine mammals, like whales and walruses, to survive, as they have for thousands of years. They bring their catch ashore to share with their neighbors. Even though the hunters use as much of the animals as they can for food and

supplies, their leftover scraps sometimes tempt polar bears looking for an easy meal.

The people know that hungry shore-bound bears will come to scavenge anything they can find after hunters have removed what they need. When the bears come into town, parents teach their children to respect the bears and to stay away from them.

FOLKTALES AND LEGENDS

There are many names for the polar bear. Each name reflects a respect and understanding of this mighty Arctic white bear. The Russian name, *beliy medved,* simply means "white bear." Norse poets praised the bears for possessing the strength of 12 men and the wit of 11. They knew the bear as "white sea deer," "rider of icebergs," and "the sailor of the floe." In parts of Greenland the bear is known as Tornassuk, meaning "the master of helping spirits." The Sami of Norway will not speak directly of the bear for fear of offending it, but refer to it as "God's dog." The Inuit speak of the polar bear in their poetry as Pihoqahiak, meaning "the ever wandering one."

A polar bear skin hangs to dry in the Inupiat Eskimo village of Shishmaref in Alaska. The skin will be used to make clothing.

All of these people learned to live among the polar bears. Growing up in an indigenous Arctic culture means learning about the Arctic environment surrounding you—and about the polar bears in your own backyard.

Legends like the Inuit tale of the woman who adopted a polar bear teach children to respect polar bears for their strength and courage. The tale shows us the deep relationship that exists between bears and humans.

According to the legend, it was Nanuk the polar bear who first taught humans how to hunt for seals. Inuit shamans, known as *angakkuit,* often call on the spirit of the polar bear, recognizing it as a powerful spiritual animal. The bears are respected, but they are also hunted as part of the northern way of life.

HUNTING THE POLAR BEAR

Hunting a polar bear, or any Arctic animal, is not taken lightly by indigenous cultures. Ceremonies and rituals honor hunters while also showing gratitude toward

The polar bear, believed to be wise and powerful, is prized by Native hunters. They pay respect to its soul by hanging its skin in a special place.

POLAR THE TITANIC BEAR

Like many children, seven-year-old Douglas Spedden owned a stuffed polar bear. The Steiff Company made it in Germany and Douglas's family bought it for him as a Christmas gift in New York City at the famous FAO Schwarz toy store in 1912. He named the stuffed animal Polar. Douglas was a very lucky boy. He traveled to many places with his parents and took Polar with him. This was during a time when the only way to travel abroad was by ship.

Douglas and his family were coming home to America from a trip to Europe and boarded a glorious new ship, the R.M.S. *Titanic*. When the infamous ship struck an Arctic iceberg, Douglas grabbed Polar and was lowered into a lifeboat. When boarding the rescue ship, Polar ended up forgotten in the lifeboat. Fortunately, a sailor rescued the stuffed bear and delivered it to Douglas. Eighty-one years later, in 1994, the story Douglas's mother wrote as a gift for her son about his stuffed polar bear and the *Titanic* adventure—*Polar the Titanic Bear*—was published and became a worldwide hit.

EIGHT SUBPOPULATIONS OF POLAR BEARS ARE DECLINING.

polar bears for providing food and warm clothing. For some indigenous groups, hunting polar bears is also about earning a living. They sell polar bear skins and other body parts around the world.

Roughly 700 to 800 polar bears are hunted each year.

COUNTING BEARS

Although the Soviet Union had banned hunting them in the 1950s, polar bears were hunted for sport in many Arctic areas until the early 1970s. Their beautiful, warm fur was a popular commodity at trading posts. So many bears were killed that in 1973, all of the Arctic countries—Canada, Denmark, Norway, Soviet Union, and the United States—signed an agreement to limit the killing of polar bears. Norway went one step

further and banned hunting altogether.

Over the years, more restrictions were established. Quotas were put in place limiting the number of bears that could be killed each year. Hunting limits allowed some polar bear populations to increase, but by the 1990s sea-ice loss caused by global warming began to set back any progress that had been made. In 2008, polar bears were listed as threatened by the United States under the Endangered Species Act.

In some areas, the indigenous people of Canada believe polar bear population counts conducted by scientists are too low and want to change the quotas. Counting polar bears is tricky because they travel vast distances and move from one population to another. Scientists attribute the increased sightings of bears in some areas to the reduction of sea ice that has forced the bears inland and into areas more populated by people.

Scientists and indigenous people don't always agree on the polar bear status and population findings. Although hunting remains a scientific and political issue in the Arctic region, everyone agrees that the polar bear population needs careful monitoring so that if changes in management need to happen, they can.

IF THE EARTH WARMS 5.4°F (3°C), THE NORTH POLE COULD BE ICE-FREE DURING THE SUMMER MONTHS.

PROTECTING POLAR BEARS

It's not enough for us to rely on governments to do the job for us when it comes to protecting polar bears. Indeed, governments can set regulations and quotas, but everybody has the ability to make a difference in the lives of polar bears—wherever they live. Scientists have pointed to climate change as the biggest threat to the polar bear population. In fact, that is the reason they were listed as threatened under the Endangered Species Act. If we all change our behaviors and use less carbon-based energy, we could see a difference. We could save polar bears!

Step it Up, Congress! Cut Carbon 80% by 2050

www.themmob.org

Environmentalists hold a rally to bring awareness to global warming.

THE TOWER OF LONDON'S POLAR BEAR

London's famous tower may have seen its share of prisoners, but not many know it was once home to a menagerie of exotic animals, including a polar bear! The famous polar bear was a gift to King Henry III from the King of Norway, Haakon IV, in 1252. It was the very first polar bear ever seen in the kingdom.

The bear arrived with a keeper, and the sheriffs of the City of London allotted about a tuppence—two pennies—to care for it. The polar bear lived in the tower with the royal menagerie of other animals, which included lions, monkeys, and an African elephant.

The small bear cub was considered lucky at the London castle, but it soon grew larger and became more expensive to feed. The tower was close to the River Thames, and it was decided by the sheriffs that the bear could catch its own food. It was given a leash and was tethered at the banks of the river so that it could bathe and catch its own salmon!

CREATE BEAR ART

Polar bears are really big—much bigger than most people realize. An adult male can weigh 1,500 pounds (700 kg) and grow almost 10 feet (3 m) long. They are the largest living nonaquatic predator. It is not until you see the size of a polar bear in person that you understand how big they really are.

Do this challenge and you will help people see how big polar bears can be.

MAKE

CREATE POLAR BEAR POSTERS

MEASURE THE SIZE OF A POLAR BEAR onto a very large piece of paper. You may need to tape together pieces of white wallpaper or craft paper to make the paper big enough.

DRAW THE OUTLINE OF THE BEAR onto the paper as accurately as you can. You could do this freehand or use a projector to shine a picture of a bear onto your paper. You could use your first bear as a template to make more.

CUT YOUR POLAR BEAR OUT of the paper as carefully and accurately as you can.

ACT

TAKE ACTION BY MAKING ART

You could:
USE PAINT, RECYCLED MATERIAL, OR SCRAP PAPER to cover your polar bear poster. Take your time to make the bear look really fantastic.

ORGANIZE A SMALL EVENT and invite people to make and paint their own polar bear posters.

ON STICKY NOTES, WRITE ACTIVITIES people could do to help polar bears. Cover the polar bear poster with the sticky notes for people to take off and do later.

SHARE

PUT YOUR POLAR BEAR POSTERS ON DISPLAY

HOLD A POLAR BEAR POSTER EXHIBITION at your school, local library, or other public space. You could put them up in places where you would not expect to see a bear. Invite people to come and see all of the different polar bears people have made.

MAKE SIGNS that clearly explain the project's mission. Include an action that you would like everyone to do that will help your campaign, like signing a petition, donating money, or reducing their contribution to climate change.

ASK EVERYONE TO PHOTOGRAPH THE BEAR POSTERS and share the pictures with their friends and family.

Here are some great ideas to get your artwork seen by lots of people:

1 Take your polar bear poster on a walk through your community. Your walking exhibition is bound to get noticed.

2 Proud of your artwork? Ask if you can have it permanently painted onto a brick wall on the side of your school.

3 Do something extreme: Make your bear 3-D by building it out of papier-mâché, snow, sand, wood, or other material.

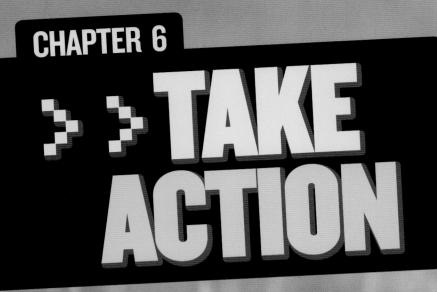

CHAPTER 6

>> TAKE ACTION

"GLOBAL WARMING ISN'T A CRISIS THAT'S DECADES AWAY. IT'S HERE NOW. THE SAD TRUTH IS THAT POLAR BEARS ARE ALREADY STARVING AS GLOBAL WARMING MELTS THE ARCTIC."

—KASSIE SIEGEL, ENVIRONMENTAL LAWYER

Two sibling cubs play and wrestle together in Canada's Hudson Bay.

Polar bears serve as an "ambassador" or "flagship" species for the Arctic. They help us see what is happening there. By learning about the stress on their population, we learn more about the effects of climate change and polar bear management.

As we watch climate change affect the polar bear population and the Arctic environment, we know it will also impact the rest of the world. If we can help conserve polar bears by limiting the change in our climate, we can also improve conservation across the planet.

ARCTIC AMBASSADOR

Siku, a captive polar bear in Denmark, is a real live Arctic ambassador. Siku's name is a common Inuit word for sea ice. Polar Bears International has paired with the Scandinavian Wildlife Park to help Siku bring attention to the Arctic environment. You can even check the young bear out on the park's Siku Cam while learning all about what you can do to help reduce your carbon footprint on its My Planet My Part website. There are tons of things you can do without even stepping out of your home!

TAKE ACTION FROM A DISTANCE

We use energy every day in the form of electricity or fuel. Every time we burn fossil fuels like oil and gas, we produce greenhouse-gas emissions that contribute to our changing climate. The more we burn, the more damage we do. Right now, climate change is the single biggest threat to polar bear survival.

We already see polar bear populations showing signs of stress. Our goal should be to keep the stresses from getting worse. It is possible to lower emissions and help curb climate change. We can encourage the use of clean, renewable energy. Carpooling or riding a bike, keeping the thermostat `set lower, and unplugging idle electronics may seem unimportant, but these measures make a difference, especially when whole communities join in.

Siku plays with a big rattle in Ouwehand Zoo in the Netherlands.

POLLUTION CARRIED ON THE WIND FROM ALL OVER THE WORLD SETTLES ON ARCTIC SNOW AND ICE. CALLED PCBs, THEY ARE FOUND IN THE BLUBBER OF POLAR BEARS.

Polar bears shake water from their coats just like dogs.

THE GREEN DREAM

Jenna Whitney's sixth-grade students at South Allegheny Elementary School jumped at the chance to help polar bears, even though McKeesport, Pennsylvania, U.S.A., is a long way from the Arctic.

Her group of five sixth graders formed the school's third Project Polar Bear team. Calling themselves the Green Dream Team, they met weekly and thought of community projects and initiatives to encourage living greener lives. Their result: They won Polar Bears International's 2013–2014 Project Polar Bear contest!

The Green Dream Team knew they could make an impact on the Arctic even though they lived far away. They started out the year sponsoring a campaign and continued by hosting a "green" holiday dinner with local foods. Serving local food not only helped the local economy, it helped save energy that would be used in transportation.

After the dinner, the team gave a presentation about polar bears and instructed guests on how they could *(continued on p. 101)*

The Project Polar Bear team members at Allegheny Elementary School show off their activism skills.

>> EXPLORER INTERVIEW

NORBERT ROSING

BORN: GERMANY
JOB TITLE: WILDLIFE AND NATURE PHOTOGRAPHER
AFFILIATIONS: POLAR BEARS INTERNATIONAL AND OTHER ORGANIZATIONS
JOB LOCATIONS: THE CANADIAN ARCTIC; CHURCHILL AND MANITOBA, CANADA; ALASKA, U.S.A.; AND THE HIGH ARCTIC OF EUROPE (ISLAND OF SPITSBERGEN)
YEARS PHOTOGRAPHING POLAR BEARS: 25

How are you helping to save polar bears?
I make people more aware of the dangers of global warming and ocean pollution by giving slide presentations and by making books of polar bear and Arctic photography.

What was your best day in the field?
For an entire day I was watching a polar bear mother with triplets. She was resting and playing with her kids. In the evening, after she nursed her cubs, she stood up. The evening light hit her and her babies. The little guys played with ice. The smallest one went right underneath its mother. The whole scene was in golden evening light. This was one of my best moments in years.

What was your worst day in the field?
I was sitting behind a blind made out of snow with a friend while we waited for a polar bear mother to emerge from her den. We were sitting there from sunrise to sunset. We sat there for five days and nothing happened. On the sixth morning we saw tracks leaving the den. She had left with her twins that night. Bad luck for us. We missed them, but wished them good luck.

How can kids prepare to do your job one day?
It really helps to live in the Arctic if you want to prepare for this job. It is not easy and it takes a long time to adjust, but eventually you adopt the spirit of the Arctic. Then you'll be prepared!

Photographer
Norbert Rosing's tips
for studying polar bears:

1 Learn everything
you can about polar
bears from books, DVDs,
exhibitions, and people
who have studied bears.

2 Get used to the
Arctic climate
and environment.

3 Become independent
from using electronic
devices for at least a
couple days. You won't
have service.

**Photographer Norbert Rosing
watching polar bears through his
camera lens behind ice blocks**

>> ANIMAL RESCUE!

FIELD AMBASSADORS SPREAD THE NEWS

Not everyone can visit the Arctic to learn about polar bears. Many of us see polar bears at zoos around the world. Fortunately, many zoos now have a field ambassador who has spent time observing polar bears in the tundra.

Polar Bears International has a unique program that brings zoo professionals to Churchill, Manitoba, where they live two weeks in the fall during polar bear season. The zoo professionals work in Churchill, helping visitors learn fun facts about polar bears. Then they bring back their experiences to their home zoos across the country, where they share them with their hometowns.

JoAnne Simerson, animal behavior enrichment manager at the St. Louis Zoo and a Polar Bear Advisory Council member, has created this program specifically for young female zoo professionals. The program, emphasizing leadership skills, has hosted ten women already from such zoos as the San Diego Zoo, Columbus Zoo, Brookfield Zoo, and Milwaukee Zoo.

Not only do these field ambassadors help teach us all about polar bears when they get home to their zoos, they also work on tree-planting campaigns and other community activities that promote green living, which ultimately helps polar bears and us!

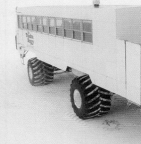

POLAR BEAR DAY

Polar Bears International's Polar Bear Day takes place every year on February 27, but you can make any day Polar Bear Day. Here's how:

ADJUST YOUR THERMOSTAT (DOWN IN THE COLDER MONTHS, UP IN THE WARMER MONTHS) TO CONSERVE ENERGY.

VOLUNTEER TO MAKE AN ARCTIC BOOK DISPLAY IN YOUR SCHOOL LIBRARY.

RECYCLE AND BUY ITEMS WITH LESS PACKAGING TO PREVENT POLLUTION FROM HITTING THE ARCTIC SHORES.

reduce their own carbon footprint. The team also collected $150 in quarters for polar bears, hosted a Power Down Day at their school, and sold over 200 "I Love Polar Bears" T-shirts. They increased local awareness and may have inspired others to take action.

They certainly made a difference!

A GROUP EFFORT

Groups everywhere are getting involved in protecting the Arctic environment. Polar bears are all around Sparta, Wisconsin, U.S.A. Well, make that polar "bearrels"—white recycling bins painted to resemble polar bears. The bins are part of an effort by Sparta High School's Earth Club to curb climate change and help save polar bears' frozen habitat.

Each school year since 2009, club members harvest about five tons of recyclable bottles and cans from the polar bearrels. The money they earn from recycling the materials goes into a polar bear

SALT WATER FREEZES AT 28.7°F (-1.8°C), ABOUT 3 DEGREES COOLER THAN FRESH WATER.

fund, which is spent on eco-friendly needs for the Sparta community to further curb climate change.

The Earth Club also reaches out to other schools and businesses to encourage recycling and saving energy throughout the community. Their endeavor caught the attention of Polar Bears International, which gave the Earth Club grant money to plant 600 trees, which soak up excess carbon dioxide, in and around Sparta.

The Sparta High School Earth Club used their creativity and enthusiasm to create a project that will help not only the polar bears' environment, but also the entire planet.

MORE WAYS TO HELP

There are other groups working just as hard. Middle school students in Ohio, U.S.A., encouraged community residents to compost at their local community garden. Another group in Utah collected food and drink wrappers and turned them into recycled crafts.

A polar bear floating in the icy Arctic in search of prey

>> **MEET A POLAR BEAR**

ANANA

Anana, Lincoln Park Zoo's polar bear, had to be kept inside during Chicago's record cold temperatures in January 2014. It was hard to believe the temperatures were even too cold for a polar bear, but Anana isn't acclimated to the polar climate anymore. The extra insulation she would carry around in the Arctic from eating seals and whales would cause her to be very uncomfortable during the year in Chicago, so the bear is fed a different diet.

Anana is used to the extreme hot and cold temperatures that normally occur in Illinois, but the polar vortex that arrived in the United States that winter made the weather unseasonably frigid—much too cold for even Chicago's polar bear!

It's hard to believe sometimes that the planet is getting warmer when we have such cold temperatures. But cold weather can still happen in the warming climate we are experiencing around the world. Scientists believe that climate change may lead to more extremes and deviations in the jet stream. In January, when Anana was experiencing the frigid temperatures in Chicago, Homer, Alaska, was experiencing record-high temperatures of 54°F (12°C).

POLAR BEAR SPY

Anthony Pagano is a spy—a polar bear spy. He doesn't dress up in a furry white costume and try to blend in, but he does get information from some pretty cool places. Make that *cold* places . . .

Pagano is a polar bear researcher with the U.S. Geological Survey in Alaska. He says spying on polar bears is the best way to learn what they do and how much energy they spend each day. Nobody knows exactly what polar bears do way out on the sea ice—especially during the dark days of the Arctic winter. It is too cold for a campout and too dark for binoculars. Radio collars tell researchers where polar bears go and how quickly they get there, but otherwise the information is limited. Pagano's new spy gadget could be a game changer.

Pagano outfits female bears with a high-tech necklace. Each collar carries a monitor that records 25 actions per second onto a computer chip to create a diary of daily activities. After one year, the collar automatically releases. Pagano retrieves the spy gear and decodes the data. He says that knowing what polar bears are doing while out of sight will help us understand the impact of climate change on their behavior.

All of these groups have organized sustainable projects, reduced greenhouse-gas emissions, and encouraged long-term change in their community. With some inspiration, you can also take action wherever you live.

But community efforts are just part of the solution. In order to have an impact, we also need to support the use of clean energy like solar and wind power throughout the world. Laws that protect polar bears from hunting, drilling, and mining need to be enforced.

You can help! Write to your local, state, and federal lawmakers to tell them you would like to see changes in how we use energy.

Remember, polar bears can't speak for themselves. The more people who speak out, the stronger the voice!

Every polar bear needs our help for their species to recover.

>> RESCUE ACTIVITIES

MAKE

POLAR BEAR PUPPET SHOW

How many of your friends have a stuffed polar bear? Perhaps more than you think. Far fewer will understand the problems that polar bears face.

By reading this book, you now know far more about polar bears than the vast majority of people on our planet. You can use this knowledge to take actions that will help polar bears and their habitats.

This final activity challenges you to tell the polar bear's story to help more people understand how they too can help these magnificent creatures.

GET INTO A TEAM AND CREATE A SHADOW PUPPET THEATER

RESEARCH a true story about a polar bear. The story should say something that will help your campaign. You could look online, watch a film, or simply pick a story from inside this book.

CUT YOUR CHARACTERS, SET, AND PROPS OUT of card paper. You could include bears, people, ice, seals, and anything else that might appear in your story.

MAKE YOUR SHADOW THEATER by shining a light against a large sheet. Be careful not to use any hot lights.

ACT

TURN YOUR STORY INTO A PLAY

TAKE SOME TIME TO PLAY AROUND with your shadow puppets behind the screen. Make sure each member of your team has a chance to stand on both sides of the screen to see how the puppets work.

TURN YOUR STORY INTO A SIMPLE SCRIPT. Decide who will play each of the characters.

PRACTICE YOUR PLAY until you are ready to give a public performance.

SHARE

PUT ON YOUR PERFORMANCE

MAKE TICKETS AND INVITE PEOPLE to come to your shadow-puppet performance. You could include key facts about polar bears on the backs of the tickets for people to read.

BEFORE STARTING, GIVE A BRIEF INTRODUCTION and explain why you have made the play.

AFTER YOUR PLAY HAS FINISHED, EXPLAIN TO YOUR AUDIENCE how they can help polar bears. You could ask them to use less energy, sign a petition, or make a donation to a charity.

SAVE THE POLAR BEARS

SHADOW PUPPET THEATRE

TICKET

ADMISSION = $5

>> BECOME AN EXPERT

There are many professionals who work directly and indirectly with polar bears. Study well, and in the future you could do one of these jobs:

CONSERVATIONIST
These professionals work to conserve habitats, including the areas where polar bears live.

GEOGRAPHER
Geographers research how people, wildlife, and habitats are interrelated. They help governments and charities make big decisions to help polar bears.

JOURNALIST
You could become a photographer, filmmaker, or a reporter, recording and sharing polar bear stories. Who knows, maybe you will even get a job with National Geographic one day!

A large polar bear inspects a tundra buggy and its driver in Churchill, Manitoba, evidence of how close humans and polar bears are today.

I t's November. Many of the ecotourists have gone home. Hudson Bay is freezing, but not quick enough. The later it freezes, the less hunting time Dancer will have. He is getting anxious. He's been on land for about four months in Churchill this year. He needs to return to hunting to build up his fat supply again.

He walks over to one of the buggies and presses his nose against the glass to get a good look inside, startling the scientist leaning her back against the window. With his strength he could easily break the glass, but he doesn't. He's just curious.

He's one of the few bears left in Churchill. Most of the younger and lighter bears have set out across the ice already, but Dancer stays behind a little longer. He waits for the temperatures to fall even further.

By mid-month, Dancer feels the familiar Arctic winter cold arriving. He sniffs the cool air. He knows that the ice is ready to support his big, heavy body. And the seals are out there to be hunted.

Just as he came, he now turns his back on the Tundra Buggies and lumbers off into the distance. Dancer returns to the ice and landscape he knows so well, for another hunting season.

Dancer lies on the snow, observing the other bears in Churchill, Manitoba, before he heads back onto the ice.

>> RESOURCES

WANT TO LEARN MORE?
Check out these great resources to continue your mission to save polar bears!

IN PRINT

Derocher, Andrew E., and Wayne Lynch. ***Polar Bears: A Complete Guide to Their Biology and Behavior***. Baltimore: Johns Hopkins University Press, 2012.

Domico, Terry. ***Bears of the World***. New York: Facts on File, 1988.

Marsh, Laura. National Geographic Reader: ***Polar Bears*** (Level 2). Washington, D.C.: National Geographic, 2013.

Newman, Mark. ***Polar Bears***. New York: Henry Holt, 2010.

Ovsyanikov, Nikita. ***Polar Bears***. Stillwater, Minnesota: Voyageur, 1998.

Ovsyanikov, Nikita. ***Polar Bears: Living With the White Bear***. Shrewsbury, U.K.: Airlife, 1996.

Rosing, Norbert. ***The World of the Polar Bear***. Richmond Hill, Ontario: Firefly, 2006.

Rosing, Norbert, and Elizabeth Carney. ***Face to Face With Polar Bears***. Washington, D.C.: National Geographic, 2007.

Spedden, Daisy Corning Stone. ***Polar the Titanic Bear***. New York: Little Brown Young Readers, 1994.

WATCH

Arctic Bears. Nature. PBS. Prod. Mark Fletcher. 2007.

Chasing Ice. National Geographic Channel. Prod. Jerry Aronson, dir. Jeff Orlowski, perf. James Balog. 2012.

In Search of Polar Bears. Culture Unplugged. Prod. Antony Jinman. 2010.

Inside Nature's Giants: Polar Bear. PBS. Prod. Mark Evans. 2009.

Polar Bear Alcatraz. Mutual of Omaha's Wild Kingdom. Perf. Dr. Nikita Ovsyanikov, Simo Barritt, Arne Naevra. 2006.

Polar Bear Alert. National Geographic. Perf. Jason Robards. 1987.

Polar Bear Mom and Cubs. National Geographic. video .nationalgeographic.com/video/bear_polar_momsandcubs.

Polar Bears, Spy on Ice. Animal Planet. Prod. John Downer. March 2011.

To the Arctic. IMAX. Prod. Christopher Palmer and Greg Foster, perf. Meryl Streep. 2012.

Top 20 Polar Bear Videos. animalplanet.com/tv-shows/other/videos/polar-bear-videos.htm.

ONLINE

IUCN/SSC Polar Bear Specialist Group
A group of research scientists from the five polar bear nations who have signed the International Agreement on the Conservation of Polar Bears.
pbsg.npolar.no

National Research Defense Council
Focusing on the polar bear's habitat.
nrdc.org

Pew's Arctic Ocean Program
Working to protect the Arctic ecosystem and its peoples.
Pewtrusts.org

Polar Conservation Organization
Providing education and outreach to conserve and sustain the polar regions.
polarconservation.org

Save the Arctic
A Greenpeace organization dedicated to conserving the Arctic.
savethearctic.org

Wildlife Conservation Society
Working to save wildlife and wild places across the globe.
wcs.org

World Wildlife Fund
Providing information on global warming and climate change, as well as conservation of the Arctic.
wwf.panda.org

SELECT SCIENTIFIC PAPERS

Amstrup, S.C., E.T. DeWeaver, et al. "Greenhouse Gas Mitigation Can Reduce Sea-Ice Loss and Increase Polar Bear Persistence." *Nature* 468 (2010), 955-58.

Amstrup, S.C., I. Stirling, et al. "Allocating Harvests Among Polar Bear Stocks in the Beaufort Sea." *Arctic* vol. 58, no. 3 (September 2005): 247-59.

Bonn, Dorothy. "Polar Bears Under Threat as Arctic Ice Melts." *Frontiers in Ecology and the Environment* 1.1 (2003): 10.

Derocher, A.E., et al. "Rapid Ecosystem Change and Polar Bear Conservation." *Conservation Letters* (January 2013): 368-375.

Dybas, Cheryl Lyn. "Polar Bears Are in Trouble—and Ice Melt's Not the Half of It." *BioScience* 62.12 (2012): 1014-018.

Holleman, M. "What Happens When Polar Bears Leave." *Interdisciplinary Studies in Literature and Environment* 14.2 (2007): 183-94.

Lubick, Naomi. "Mercury Levels on the Rise in Polar Bears." *Chemical & Engineering News* (January 10, 2011): DOI: 010611151713.

Overeem, Irina. "Polar Bears: The Natural History of a Threatened Species." *Arctic, Antarctic, and Alpine Research* 45.3 (2013): 423-24.

Ovsyanikov, Nikita. "Polar Bears: Living With the White Bear." *The American Biology Teacher* 60.3 (1998): 235-36.

Post, E., et al. "Ecological Consequences of Sea-Ice Decline." *Science* 341 (August 2013): 519-524.

Stirling, I., and A.E. Derocher. "Effects of Climate Warming on Polar Bears: A Review of the Evidence." *Global Change Biology* 18 (September 2012): 2694-2706.

Stirling, Ian. "Research and Management of Polar Bears Ursus Maritimus." *Polar Record* 23.143 (1986): 167. Web.

Tyrrell, Martina. "More Bears, Less Bears: Inuit and Scientific Perceptions of Polar Bear Populations on the West Coast of Hudson Bay." *Études/Inuit/Studies* 30.2 (2006): 191.

Waterman, J.M., et al. "Can Whisker Spot Patterns Be Used to Identify Polar Bears?" *Journal of Zoology* (March 2007): DOI:10.1111/j.1469-7998.2007.00340.x.

ORGANIZATIONS FEATURED IN THIS BOOK

Polar Bears International
For more information, check out pages 19, 24, 94, and 100.
www.polarbearsinternational.org

U.S. Fish and Wildlife Service
For more information, check out pages 21 and 53.

PLACES TO SEE POLAR BEARS AROUND THE WORLD

Alaska Zoo, Anchorage, Alaska, U.S.A.
Bronx Zoo, New York, U.S.A.
Brookfield Zoo, Chicago, Illinois, U.S.A.
Churchill, Manitoba, Canada
Cincinnati Zoo & Botanical Garden, Ohio, U.S.A.
Lincoln Park Zoo, Chicago, Illinois, U.S.A.
London Zoo, England
Louisville Zoo, Kentucky, U.S.A.

Maryland Zoo, Baltimore, Maryland, U.S.A.
Milwaukee County Zoo, Wisconsin, U.S.A.
Philadelphia Zoo, Pennsylvania, U.S.A.
San Diego Zoo, California, U.S.A.
Scandinavian Wildlife Park, Denmark
Toledo Zoo, Ohio, U.S.A.
Toronto Zoo, Canada

Boldface indicates illustrations.

A
Alaska
    denning areas 57–58
    melting ice 58, 71
    oil pipeline 42, **42**
    orphaned cubs 53
    see also Homer; Shishmaref
Amstrup, Steven C. 24–25, **24–25**, 27
Anana (polar bear) 102, **102**
Arctic ecosystem 8, 23, 26
Arctic Ocean 32, 71

B
Bearded seals **64–65**, 71, **71**
Bechshoft, Thea 35, **38**, 38–39, 41
Beluga whales 24, 66, 71, **71**
Black bears **32**, 40, **40**, 50
Blubber, seal 53, 66
Body language 67, 75
Boreal forest 10
Breiter, Matthias 67, **67**
Brown bears 19, **32**, 33; *see also* Grizzly bears

C
Camouflage 20, 66
Campaigns 28–29, **28–29**, 97, 100
Canada
    indigenous people 87
    see also Churchill; Hudson Bay
Carbon dioxide 23, 76, 101
Chukchi people 83
Churchill, Manitoba, Canada 10, 23, **80–81**, 100, 107
    ecotourism 82, 107
    garbage dump 70, **70–71**
    polar bear patrol 82, **82**
Claws 22, **22**
Climate change
    carbon footprint 94, 101
    extreme weather 42, 102
    fossil fuels 26, 94
    greenhouse gases 23, 26
    rising temperatures 26, 41–42, 60, 87, 88, 92, 98
    sea-ice melting 8, 26, 36, 46, 53, 58, 73, 87–88
    as threat to polar bears 42, 89, 94
    what you can do 94, 97, 101, 103
    see also Energy, conserving; Recycling; Rescue activities
Collars, tracking 21, **21**, 53, 103
Color, fur 20, 33
Cooling down 16, 58, **58**
Cubs
    birth 16, 48, 50, 71
    learning to hunt 53
    nursing 16, 48, 50, 53
    orphans 51, 53
    play **92–93**, **94–95**

D
Dens 48, 50, **56–57**, 57–58
DNA testing 33
Doerflein, Thomas 18, **18–19**
Dog, sniffer 59, **59**

E
Ear-tag transmitters **20**
Eggs, bird 74
Endangered Species Act (1973) 41, 87, 89
Energy, conserving 60–61, 77, 100
Expert tips
    conserving energy 61, 77
    fund-raising 45
    showing artwork 91
    studying polar bears 27, 29, 57, 90
    writing petitions 29
Explorer interviews
    Nikita Ovsyanikov 54–55
    Norbert Rosing 98–99
    Sarah McNair-Landry 68–69
    Steven C. Amstrup 24–25
    Thea Bechshoft 38–39

F
Fast, summer 71, 73
Fat, insulating 19, 20, 23, 36, 50, 64, 71
Feces 59
Fireweed **34–35**
Folktales and legends 83, 85
Food chain 23, 42, 64, 66
Footpads 22, **22**
Fossil fuels 26, 94
Frazil 51, **51**
Fund-raising 44–45, **44–45**
Fur 19–20, 33, 57, 66
Fur trade 87

G
Garbage picking 70, **70**
Global warming 26, 42, 60, 87, 88, 92, 98
Greenhouse gases 23, 26, 94, 103
Greenland 32, 71, 83
Grizzly bears 33, 40, **40**
Grolar bears 33, **33**
Gus (polar bear) 72, **72–73**

H
Habitat loss 7, 33, 60
Harp seals 70, **70**
Helicopters 82, **82**
Henry VIII, King (England) 89
Hibernation 50, 57, 66
Homer, Alas.: record-high temperatures 102
Hudson Bay, Canada 10, 19, 23, **56–57**, **78–79**, **92–93**, 107
Human-bear conflicts 26
Hunters, native 41, 73, **83**, 85, **85**, 87, 88
Hunting bans 54, 87
Hybrid bears 33, **33**

I
Ice, types of 50–51, **50–51**
Ice floes 57, **62–63**
Indigenous people 83, 85, 87, 88
Inuit 83, 85
Inupiat 83, 85

K
Knut (polar bear) 18, **18–19**

L
Lawmakers 103
Long-distance swimming 44, 45, 52, 73

M
Map: polar bear range 17
Marine ecosystem 10
Marine mammals 16, 31, 83
McNair-Landry, Sarah 68–69, **68–69**
Metabolic rate 66
Methane 23, 76
Milk 16, 48, 53
Myths, polar bear 21

N
Nanuk, legend of 85
Nilas 51, **51**
North Pole 32, 71, 83, 88
Norway 43, 80, 83, 87; *see also* Svalbard

O
Operation Snowflake 53
Orphaned cubs 51, 53
Ovsyanikov, Nikita 51, **51**, 54–55, **54–55**

P
Pack ice **22–23**, 50, **50**, **64–65**, 74
Pagano, Anthony 103, **103**
Pancake ice 51, **51**
Pandas **32**, 40, **40**
Patrols, polar bear 26, 82, 83
Paws 16, **16**, 19, 21, 22, **22**
Petitions 29, 91, 105
Phylogenetic tree **32**
Pizzly bears 33, **33**
Polar, the Titanic Bear (stuffed bear) 86, **86**
Polar Bear 20741 (marathon swimmer) 52
Polar Bear Day 100
Polar bears
    counting 87–88
    in family tree **32**
    how to help 94, 97, 100, 101, 103
    see also Rescue activities
    hunting skills 53, 64, 66, 71
    listed as threatened species (2008) 24, 41, 87
    protecting 88–89, 103
    relocating 70, 82, **82**
    size and weight 35, 40, 90
    studying: expert tips 27, 29, 57, 90
    threats to 8, 41, 42, 54, 89, 94
Polar Bears International (PBI) 19, 24, 94, 97, 100, 101
Pollution 38, 41, 42, 61, 96, 98, 100
Poop 59
Pregnancy 50, 57, 59
Pressure ridges (ice) 50, **50**
Prey 70–71, **70–71**; *see also* Beluga whales; Seals; Walruses

Q
Quotas, hunting 41, 83, 87, 89

R
Radio collars 53, 103
Range map 17

Recycling 100, 101
Rescue activities
    campaigns 28–29, **28–29**
    conserving energy 60–61, **60–61**
    cookbook 76–77, **76–77**
    fund-raising 44–45, **44–45**
    posters 90–91, **90–91**
    puppet show 104–105, **104–105**
Ringed seals 16, 53, 57, 66, 70, **70**, 71
Rode, Karyn **24–25**
Rosing, Norbert 98–99, **98–99**
Russia 32, 54, 80; *see also* Wrangel Island

S

Salt water 101
Satellite transmitters 20, **20**
Scavenging 51, 74, 83
Sea ice
    melting 8, 26, 36, 46, 53, 58, 73, 87–88
    types of 50–51, **50–51**
Seals
    blubber 53, 66
    lairs 53, 70
    pups 12, 53, 57, **70**, 71
    see also Bearded seals; Harp seals; Ringed
        seals
Shishmaref, Alas.: polar bear skin **84–85**
Simerson, JoAnne 100
Smell, sense of
    dogs 59
    polar bears 66
Spedden, Douglas 86
Stuffed polar bears 44, **44**, 86, **86**
Svalbard, Norway **42–43**, 58, 87

T

Tattoos 20, **20**
Teeth 16, **20**, 32
Titanic, R.M.S. 86
Tower of London, London, England 89
Toys, polar bear 72, **72**, **94–95**
Trans-Alaska pipeline 42, **42**
Tundra Buggies 10, 12, **19**, **23**, **100**, **106–107**
Tundra ecosystem 10
Twins 33, 57

U

U.S. Fish and Wildlife Service 21, 53

W

Walking hibernation 66
Walruses 10, 16, 64, 66, 71, **71**, 74, 83
Water, metabolic 65
Waterman, Jane 23
Weather, extreme 42, 102
Whisker spot patterns 23
Wlock, Brett 82
Wrangel Island, Russia 51, **54–55**

Y

Yawning 75, **75**
Yup'iit people 83

Z

Zoos 18, 35, 53, 59, 72, **72–73**, **94–95**, 100, 109

>> IMAGE CREDITS

COVER, Matthias Breiter/Minden Pictures; back cover, Ralph Lee Hopkins/National Geographic Creative; spine, Eric Isselée/Dreamstime; 1, Design Pics Inc./National Geographic Creative; 2-3, Ralph Lee Hopkins/National Geographic Creative; 4-5 (RT), Matthias Breiter; 6 (UPLE), Marina Cano Trueba/Shutterstock; 6 (UPRT), Anup Shah/Taxi/Getty Images; 6 (CTR), Karl Ammann/Digital Vision; 6 (CTR RT), Tim Davis/Corbis; 6 (LOLE), Lisa & Mike Husar; 7 (UPLE), Tim Fitzharris; 7 (CTR LE), SecondShot/Shutterstock; 7 (LOLE), Matthias Breiter/ Minden Pictures; 7 (RT), Darren Moore; 8-9 (RT), Matthias Breiter; 10-11 (RT), Karine Genest/nature360degrees.com); 12-13 (RT), Kelsey Eliasson/polarbearalley.com; 12 (LORT), Dr. Jane M. Waterman; 14-15, Design Pics Inc./National Geographic Creative; 7, National Geographic Maps; 18-19 (LE), Sean Gallup/Staff/Getty Images; 19 (LORT), CB2/ZOB/Newscom; 20 (LORT), Uzi Eszterhas/Minden Pictures/National Geographic Creative; 20 (LOCTR), Norbert Rosing/National Geographic Creative; 21 (UP), Terry Biddle; 21 (LOLE), Paul J. Richards/Getty Images; 22 (UPLE), Daniel J Cox/Getty Images; 22, Jim Brandenburg/National Geographic Creative; 23 (LORT), CB2/ZOB/Newscom; 24-25, Daniel J. Cox/Corbis; 24 (UPRT), Kt Miller/polarbearsinternational.org; 26-27 (RT), Rinie Van Meurs/Foto Natura/MI/National Geographic Creative; 28 (LO), Daniel Raven-Ellison; 28 (UPRT), Daniel Raven-Ellison; 28-29, Ansis Klucis/Shutterstock; 29, Daniel Raven-Ellison; 29 (UP CTR), Steven Kazlowski/naturepl.com; 30-31, Matthias Breiter; 32 (A), Universal Images Group Limited/Alamy; 32 (B), Universal Images Group Limited/Alamy; 32 (C), The Natural History Museum/Alamy; 32 (D), Roger Hall/Science Source; 32 (E), Universal Images Group Limited/Alamy; 32 (F), The Natural History Museum/Alamy; 32 (G), Universal Images Group Limited/Alamy; 32 (H), The Natural History Museum/Alamy; 32 (I), Universal Images Group Limited/Alamy; 32 (J), Universal Images Group Limited/Alamy; 32 (K), Universal Images Group Limited/Alamy; 32 (L), Universal Images Group Limited/Alamy; 33, Steven J. Kazlowski/Alamy; 34-35 (LE), Matthias Breiter/Minden Pictures; 34 (UPLE), Nick Garbutt/Getty Images; 36-37 (UPRT), Design Pics Inc/National Geographic Creative; 36 (LOCTR), Norbert Rosing/National Geographic Creative; 36 (LORT), Henrik Sorensen/Getty Images; 37 (LOLE), Norbert Rosing/Contributor/Getty Images; 37 (LORT), Steven Kazlowski/Minden Pictures; 38 (UP CTR), Kt Miller/polarbearsinternational.org; 38-39 (RT), Matthias Breiter; 40 (UPRT), Donald M. Jones/Getty Images; 40 (UPLE), Pete Ryan/Getty Images; 40 (CTR RT), Suzi Eszterhas/Minden Pictures/National Geographic Creative; 40 (LOLE), Bob Smith/National Geographic Creative; 41 (LO), Courtesy of the University of Alberta; 42 (CTR), Michael S. Quinton/National Geographic Creative; 42-43 (RT), Ira Block/National Geographic Creative; 44 (LE), Daniel Raven-Ellison; 44 (UF), Daniel Raven-Ellison; 44-45, Ansis Klucis/Shutterstock; 46-47, Paul Nicklen/National Geographic Creative; 48-49 (RT), Norbert Rosing/National Geographic Creative; 48 (LOCTR), Danita Delimont/Getty Images; 50 (CTR), Norbert Wu/Minden Pictures/National Geographic Creative; 50 (LOLE), Borge Ousland/National Geographic Creative; 51 (CTR RT), E. R. Degginger/Alamy; 51 (LORT), Bryan and Cherry Alexander/Science Source; 51 (LOLE), Steve and Donna O'Meara/National Geographic Creative; 52, Paul Souders/Getty Images; 53 (LORT), Anchorage Daily News/Contributor/Getty Images; 54 (UPRT), Irina Menyushina; 54-55 (RT), Irina Menyushina; 56-57 (LE), Thorsten Milse/Getty Images; 58 (CTR), Design Pics Inc./National Geographic Creative; 58 (LORT), Paul Nicklen/National Geographic Creative; 58 (LOLE), Mitsuaki Iwago/Minden Pictures/National Geographic Creative; 59, Orlin Wagner/AP/Corbis; 60 (LO), Norbert Rosing/National Geographic Creative; 60 (UPRT), Daniel Raven-Ellison; 60-61, Ansis Klucis/Shutterstock; 61 (CTF), James Ingram/Alamy; 62-63, Pal Hermansen/Getty Images; 64-65 (RT), Wayne Lynch/Getty Images; 64 (LOLE), Fred Bruemmer/Getty Images; 66 (LO), Terry Biddle; 67, S. J. Krasemann/Getty Images; 67 (UPRT), Matthias Breiter/Minden Pictures/National Geographic Creative; 68 (CTR RT), Erik Boomer; 68-69, Eric McNair-Landry; 70 (UPLE), Jenny E. Ross/Corbis; 70 (LOLE), AleksandrN/Shutterstock; 70 (LORT), zanskar/iStockphoto; 71 (RT CTR), Brian J. Skerry/National Geographic Creative; 71 (LOLE), Thorsten Milse/Getty Images; 71 (LO), pum_eva/iStockphoto; 72-73 (RT), New York Daily News Archive/Contributor/Getty Images; 73 (UPRT), New York Daily News Archive/Contributor/Getty Images; 74 (LO), Doug Allan/Minden Pictures; 75 (CTR LE), Redmond Durrell/Alamy; 75 (UPRT), Steven J. Kazlowski/Alamy; 75 (LORT), Paul Nicklen/National Geographic Creative; 76 (LOLE), Daniel Raven-Ellison; 76 (UPRT), Daniel Raven-Ellison; 76-77, Ansis Klucis/Shutterstock; 77 (LOLE), Nick Norman/National Geographic Creative; 77 (CTR), Daniel Raven-Ellison; 78-79, Ingrid Visser/Minden Pictures; 80 (LOLE), John Zada/Alamy; 80-81 (RT), Matthias Breiter/Getty Images; 80, Matthias Breiter; 80 (CTR LE), Matthias Breiter; 83 (UP), David Coventry/National Geographic Creative; 84-85 (LE), Doug Allan/Getty Images; 86, Steiff GmbH; 86, Mark Thiessen, NGS; 87 (UP), Richard Sidey - RichardSidey.com/Getty Images; 88 (LO), Green Stock Media/Alamy; 88, Philip Pound/Alamy; 90 (CTR LE), Sergey Uryadnikov/Alamy; 90 (UPRT), Daniel Raven-Ellison; 90-91, Ansis Klucis/Shutterstock; 91 (LOLE), Daniel Raven-Ellison; 92-93, Nick Garbutt/Getty Images; 94-95 (RT), Koen Van Weel/epa/Corbis; 96-97 (LE), Flip Nicklin/Minden Pictures/National Geographic Creative; 96-97 (LORT), Jenna Whitney; 98-99, Norbert Rosing/National Geographic Creative; 100 (LO), Terry Biddle; 100 (UPLE), Daniel J. Cox/NaturalExposures.com; 100 (UPLE), Daniel J. Cox/NaturalExposures.com; 101 (LO), Ralph Lee Hopkins/National Geographic Creative; 102 (CTR), Yan-chun Tung/Getty Images; 103 (UPRT), Mike Lockhart, USGS; 103 (LORT), Mitsuaki Iwago/Minden Pictures; 104 (UPRT), Daniel Raven-Ellison; 104 (CTR LE), Daniel Raven-Ellison; 104-105, Ansis Klucis/Shutterstock; 105 (LOCTR), Daniel Raven-Ellison; 106-107 (LE), Flip Nicklin/Minden Pictures/National Geographic Creative; 107 (LORT), Dr. Jane M. Waterman; 108 (LOLE), Norbert Rosing/National Geographic Creative; 109 (CTR RT), Flip Nicklin/Minden Pictures

From page 7: $10.00 donation to National Geographic Society. Charges will appear on your wireless bill or be deducted from your prepaid balance. All purchases must be authorized by account holder. Must be 18 years of age or have parental permission to participate. Message and data rates may apply. Text STOP to 50555 to STOP. Text HELP to 50555 for HELP. Full terms: www.mGive.org/T

For the little ones, Teagan, Ellie, and Bishop. May you always know there are polar bears in the wild. —N. C.

To the polar bears who are surviving in the changing Arctic. —K. S.

For Seb, Menah, Mushroom, and all Earthlings. —D. R.

Many thanks to Jennifer Emmett, Kate Olesin, JR Mortimer, Daniel Raven-Ellison, and the entire National Geographic Kids Books team who helped make this book possible.

Special thanks to all the explorers, researchers, conservationists, and organizations that have dedicated themselves to protecting polar bears and were featured within these pages. Your stories, photos, and expertise were invaluable. Particular thanks to Steven Amstrup for reviewing this book for accuracy. —N. C.

Thanks to all of those who are working hard to save polar bears in their natural habitat. —K. S.

Copyright © 2014 National Geographic Society

All rights reserved. Reproduction of the whole or any part of the contents without written permission from the publisher is prohibited.

Published by the National Geographic Society

Gary E. Knell, *President and Chief Executive Officer*
John M. Fahey, *Chairman of the Board*
Declan Moore, *Executive Vice President; President, Publishing and Travel*
Melina Gerosa Bellows, *Publisher; Chief Creative Officer, Books, Kids, and Family*

Prepared by the Book Division

Hector Sierra, *Senior Vice President and General Manager*
Nancy Laties Feresten, *Senior Vice President, Kids Publishing and Media*
Eva Absher-Schantz, *Design Director, Kids Publishing and Media*
Jay Sumner, *Director of Photography, Kids Publishing*
Jennifer Emmett, *Vice President, Editorial Director, Kids Books*
R. Gary Colbert, *Production Director*
Jennifer A. Thornton, *Director of Managing Editorial*

Staff for This Book

Kate Olesin, *Editor*
JR Mortimer, *Project Manager*
Julide Dengel, *Art Director*
Graves Fowler Creative, *Designer*
Lori Epstein, *Senior Photo Editor*
Bri Bertoia, *Special Projects Assistant*
Paige Towler, *Editorial Assistant*
Sanjida Rashid, *Design Production Assistant*
Margaret Leist, *Photo Assistant*
Carl Mehler, *Director of Maps*
Sven M. Dolling, *Map Research and Production*
Grace Hill, *Associate Managing Editor*
Joan Gossett, *Production Editor*
Lewis R. Bassford, *Production Manager*
Susan Borke, *Legal and Business Affairs*

Production Services

Phillip L. Schlosser, *Senior Vice President*
Chris Brown, *Vice President, NG Book Manufacturing*
George Bounelis, *Senior Production Manager*
Nicole Elliott, *Director of Production*
Rachel Faulise, *Manager*
Robert L. Barr, *Manager*

 The National Geographic Society is one of the world's largest nonprofit scientific and educational organizations. Founded in 1888 to "increase and diffuse geographic knowledge," the Society's mission is to inspire people to care about the planet. It reaches more than 400 million people worldwide each month through its official journal, National Geographic, and other magazines; National Geographic Channel; television documentaries; music; radio; films; books; DVDs; maps; exhibitions; live events; school publishing programs; interactive media; and merchandise. National Geographic has funded more than 10,000 scientific research, conservation, and exploration projects and supports an education program promoting geographic literacy.

For more information, please visit nationalgeographic.com, call 1-800-NGS LINE (647-5463), or write to the following address:
National Geographic Society
1145 17th Street N.W.
Washington, D.C. 20036-4688 U.S.A.

Visit us online at nationalgeographic.com/books

For librarians and teachers: ngchildrensbooks.org

More for kids from National Geographic: kids.nationalgeographic.com

For information about special discounts for bulk purchases, please contact National Geographic Books Special Sales: ngspecsales@ngs.org

For rights or permissions inquiries, please contact National Geographic Books Subsidiary Rights: ngbookrights@ngs.org

Paperback ISBN: 978-1-4263-1731-6
Reinforced library binding ISBN: 978-1-4263-1732-3

Printed in the United States of America
14/WOR/1